The Dog
Next Door

Other books by Callie Smith Grant

A Prince among Dogs: And Other Stories of the Dogs We Love
A Dickens of a Cat: And Other Stories of the Cats We Love

The Dog
Next Door

And Other Stories *of the* Dogs We Love

Edited *by* Callie Smith Grant

Revell

a division of Baker Publishing Group
Grand Rapids, Michigan

© 2011 by Baker Publishing Group

Published by Revell
a division of Baker Publishing Group
P.O. Box 6287, Grand Rapids, MI 49516-6287
www.revellbooks.com

Printed in the United States of America

Library of Congress Cataloging-in-Publication Data
The dog next door : and other stories of the dogs we love / edited by Callie Smith Grant.
   p. cm.
  Includes bibliographical references.
  ISBN 978-0-8007-3419-0 (pbk.)
  1. Dog owners—Religious life. 2. Dogs—Religious aspects—Christianity—Anecdotes. I. Grant, Callie Smith. II. Title: And other stories of the dogs we love.
  BV4596.A54D64 2011
  231.7—dc22
                                                    2011000887

In keeping with biblical principles of creation stewardship, Baker Publishing Group advocates the responsible use of our natural resources. As a member of the Green Press Initiative, our company uses recycled paper when possible. The text paper of this book is comprised in part of post-consumer waste.

12   13   14   15   16   17   9 8 7 6

To my husband,
a friend to dogs everywhere

Contents

Introduction

Callie Smith Grant

*M*y husband and I live on a lovely, tree-lined country road that doesn't get a lot of traffic. We see some commuters, one school bus, tractors and combines, and a few teenage kids with loud stereos thumping from their vehicles. But otherwise it's pretty quiet.

Every now and then, however, a pickup driven by an elderly gentleman goes slowly by. We know the truck because we've come to recognize the bark of its canine passenger.

No matter what season we're in—bitter winter, humid summer, and everything in between—the front passenger window is down some if not all of the way. Sitting on the truck's bench seat is a big dog who's either hanging his head out the window or trying to. Around every five seconds, he gives one big, loud, whooping bark with that underlying whine my husband and I recognized from the first as belonging to a hound of some kind. We hear this before we actually see the dog.

The truck with man and dog passes by a couple times per week. We don't know who they are or where they live, but we do know this—that is one happy hound. Whenever we hear them down the road, my husband and I stop what we're doing, look for each other, and smile. No words are necessary.

America's 44.9 million dog owners know there are myriad reasons to have a dog in their lives.[1] Dogs are good company, they protect us, they keep us on track in the daily grind, and sometimes they simply help us enjoy the world we might otherwise get too busy to appreciate. That's what I think about our drive-by hound—he reminds me that the air is fresh and the day is full of possibility.

I view the dog as one of God's finest creations. When I looked for material for this book, I wanted good, true stories about these noble beasts, stories that also might offer some perspective into why the dog came into the author's life. Some things we'll never know in this world, of course, but some reasons do present themselves clearly.

I found excellent and often powerful stories I know you will enjoy. There are stories of dogs that saved people's lives and dogs that kept children safe. Less dramatic but just as valuable are the stories of dogs that helped the aged and infirm enjoy their days. I was presented with stories of dogs that offered support to strangers in need. Some of the dogs in this book displayed uncanny abilities to know when their human was in medical trouble. There are some tributes to beloved childhood dogs. I even discovered stories of dogs that saved other dogs.

In the 1930s, the great Helen Keller—blind and deaf since infancy but nevertheless amazingly accomplished—was given an Akita by the emperor of Japan. She was the first American to acquire this stunning breed, the hometown dog of Japan. She loved her Akita dearly, and when that dog died too soon, the emperor sent her another Akita. Miss Keller called her dog "an angel in fur."[2] We lovers of dogs can understand that, can't we?

My father always dreamed of moving to a remote Greek island to live. I once told a Greek gentleman that. He pulled out a map of his homeland and said, "In Greece, there are many islands, and there's an island for everyone. Let's find one for your papa."

I'm convinced it is also true that there is the right dog for everyone.

Some of those wonderful creatures find us or are given to us—you'll read about many of those in this book. And many more dogs still wait to be found.

I sincerely hope that after you've enjoyed the stories in this book, you'll wonder about that perfect dog for you and consider finding it if you haven't already. Or even the semi-perfect dog. Or more than one dog. I also hope that you'll feel compelled to visit your local animal shelter, humane society, or rescue association and get involved with some aspect of the running of these places.

And it is my hope that you will meet that dog who is your own "angel in fur" and add it to your family. In the meantime, enjoy the stories.

A Walk of Joy

Virginia Smith

I sure would like to meet BJ."
My father's speech was difficult to understand since the stroke that left him almost completely paralyzed, but his request held an unmistakable plea. I knew the boredom of long days at the nursing home was agony for this previously active outdoorsman, and I'd do just about anything to help him relieve the tedium. But how would my ultratimid dog react to the unusual sights and sounds and smells of this place?

BJ had moved into my empty nest several months before. My husband and I weren't looking for a dog, but when the local newspaper broke the story of a raid on an area puppy mill, the plight of all those mistreated puppies touched our hearts. The rescued animals had been distributed to shelters across the state, including one in our town, so no single facility would be overburdened. We drove out there reluctantly, not sure what to expect but certainly not ready to fall in love with the matted, filthy, stinking, three-month-old black standard poodle huddled pathetically in a cold corner of the concrete pen. We instantly knew he was coming home with us.

BJ had never been around people or even inside a house. He was terrified of everything. He didn't so much cower as collapse whenever he encountered anything unfamiliar, which was just about everything for the first few weeks. We almost named him Pancake because of his habit of dropping flat to the ground in terror, but settled on BJ, short for the French salutation *bonjour*. (He was a French poodle, after all!) When he conquered one fear, something new and terrifying loomed up to take its place—toys, his food bowl, the refrigerator door, the recliner's footrest, even leaves blowing across the grass. One of his biggest fears was any terrain that inclined. Our first outdoor walk turned to disaster as we tried unsuccessfully to coax him up the very small hill at the end of our street. My husband spent weeks down on his hands and knees teaching BJ how to go up the stairs.

BJ's one great passion, after he overcame his initial terror, was for tennis balls. He was an accomplished fetcher and would chase a ball until our arms ached from throwing it for him. So when I received permission to take BJ to the nursing home to meet Daddy, I went armed with balls.

Navigating the hallway leading to my father's room was like running a gauntlet on the best of days. Wheelchairs and stretchers occupied by elderly or injured residents crowded the gleaming white halls and made a quick dash to Daddy's private room impossible. Especially with a fifty-pound chicken dog trying to wrap himself around my legs. BJ had not displayed a tendency toward aggression in the months since we adopted him, but neither had I exposed him to crowds or to more than one or two close friends at a time. I was afraid he'd react in blind terror, and there was no telling what would happen.

"Lord," I whispered, "please let us get to Daddy's room without anything bad happening."

I shortened the lead, and we began weaving our way between the dozing occupants of wheelchairs. We hadn't reached the halfway point when a loud voice rang out.

"A dog! A dog!"

We'd been spotted. Heart pounding, I saw a young man, a head injury patient with whom I was vaguely familiar, speeding toward us in his electric wheelchair. I froze. BJ froze. Aroused by the shout, one elderly face looked our way, and then another. In the next instant we were surrounded with wheelchair-bound patients, all of whom wanted to meet the big black poodle.

I squatted down and placed an arm around BJ. He was trembling, his heart thundering as hard as mine. He pressed into me as the young man zoomed right up to us and reached out with an awkward hand to pound on his back. I thought BJ would certainly cower from the rough caresses, but he stood his ground. The disabled man laughed with delight and pounded harder.

Then a nearby elderly woman held out a tentative hand. "May I pet him too?"

"Uh, sure." I led BJ to her, surprised when he came easily.

A smile lit the lady's creased face as her fingers encountered his curly fur. "He's so soft. I had a dog once. Her name was Lady."

More hands joined hers, and wheelchairs inched closer. "This one's name is BJ," I told our audience, as a half dozen people rubbed him, clearly thrilled to have a four-legged visitor. To my utter amazement, BJ not only tolerated their attention, after a moment he actually wandered from one wheelchair to the next, as though aware of the joy and pleasure he was affording the residents.

That short walk down the hallway to Daddy's room took longer than ever before, because every resident—and the staff too—wanted to pet the friendly giant poodle. I took my time, watching this refugee from a puppy mill spread happiness to those confined in a place with few joys, many of them due to circumstances beyond their control. Just as BJ had been when we found him. I saw smiles on faces where I'd previously seen only scowls or tears, and I silently promised God that I'd strive to bring those smiles back more often.

By the time BJ arrived in Daddy's room, he was prancing, his head held high, clearly having the time of his life and

The Studies Are In!

It's no news flash to dog lovers, but now studies confirm that having a dog in your life absolutely equals better health. Dog lovers knew this anyway, but isn't it nice to know science agrees? It turns out that dog owners tend to enjoy the benefits of:

- lower risk of heart disease
- lower risk of high blood pressure
- better cholesterol levels
... than they would have without their dog.

Of course you have to take your dog outside for walks and powder room trips. This means you'll most likely get up to 77 percent more exercise than you would without your canine buddy.

Need we also mention the emotional benefits of living with a creature that simply adores you? That's worth a lot in dog food!

So when do we get a discount in our health insurance for such a heart-healthy lifestyle?[3]

enormously pleased with himself. Daddy was thrilled with his grand-dog and loved watching BJ fetch the ball I rolled the short distance across the floor of his room. When I left, it was with a light heart, pondering the lesson my timid dog taught me that day. Even our most dreadful fears have no power in the face of joy. Especially when that joy is a gift we give to others.

In the years that followed, BJ became a regular visitor to Daddy's nursing home, and he was always greeted with enthusiasm. Though he remained terrified of strangers in general, he loved those people. Maybe he sensed that they loved him. Or perhaps he simply enjoyed spreading joy.

They Protect Their Children

Sherri Gallagher

I grew up in dairy country in upstate New York. The nearest neighbor was a farmer half a mile away. Dad had dreamed of raising German shepherds, and this was a place his dreams could come true. That is how I came to grow up with more four-footed than two-footed friends. My parents always claimed they raised the shepherds and the shepherds raised my sister, Virginia, and me.

Mom and Dad built a huge rambling house that fit sunny California a great deal better than it did an upstate New York winter. They were some of the original do-it-yourselfers simply because they couldn't afford to hire the work done. The land dropped a full story in the width of the driveway, and retaining walls prevented the rocks and dirt we called a lawn from reclaiming the space for cars.

Mom told me on repeated occasions that I was not a napping kind of child. I got up in the morning and went full tilt until she corralled me and put me to bed—multiple times.

One of the rare exceptions to that rule was the day I welcomed Mounty into our home. Mounty was a large, two-year-old, black-and-tan grandson of early television's famous dog Rin Tin Tin. Dad had bought him to be the foundation stud for a family kennel. My parents had talked in general terms about Dad's big dream of having a kennel, and Mom hadn't said anything against the idea. But she actually was afraid of dogs—especially big dogs. At the time Dad surprised Mom and brought Mounty home, Mom still hadn't gotten around to telling Dad about her fear. Dad ushered the dog into the kitchen and admonished Mom that the change in family had disoriented Mounty and she shouldn't scare him. Then Dad left for work. My father never realized Mom's silence was due to being scared speechless.

The groceries she'd just purchased littered the counter in front of her, and she spied the ham she'd been about to refrigerate. Grabbing a knife, she hacked off a generous chunk and tossed it to Mounty. He caught it in midair, never moving his feet. His inch-long teeth snapped shut with a clunk. A couple of moist smacks and the meat disappeared.

Theorizing a well-fed dog was less likely to make a meal of the closest human, Mom proceeded to feed the dog the whole ham, chunk by chunk. As Mounty watched her with big, sorrowful brown eyes, the ham dwindled piece by piece until only the bone was left. Tossing it with all the skill learned in her softball days, Mom then darted for the living room. Mounty caught the bone with the grace of an outfielder collecting an easy fly ball and lay down to gnaw on his treasure.

That's when I entered the picture. Standing up, I was eyeball to eyeball with Mounty as he lay down. He apparently looked like a big, soft pillow, so I toddled over and curled up to take a nap on this fur-covered cushion. Mounty wrapped around me, a living blanket, and didn't budge.

Mom said she tried to pick me up only to have her hands firmly batted away by a big black nose. The look in the dog's eyes was clear. I was not to be touched. I was his child to protect. Mom hovered there for hours while the sun slowly set and I slumbered peacefully.

Dad's return woke me, and I wandered away to play, Mounty a watchful two steps behind. Just before he followed me from the room, Mounty picked up his bone and politely dropped it on Mom's feet while slowly wagging his tail. Dad howled with laughter when Mom confessed why we were going to have a week of meatless dinners.

Sig, Signet, and Electra soon followed Mounty. Wherever I played, a protective circle of German shepherds surrounded me. When the neighbor's barn burned and every structure for miles around became infested with bold, aggressive rats, I was safe. Dad looked out the window one day and saw a rat coming across the lawn toward me as I played in the grass. He grabbed a machete and ran for the door. He got outside just in time to see Sig grab the rodent's tail and flip it into the air, snapping its back.

When I was probably three years old, a pile of sand was delivered and dumped in the middle of the driveway to be mixed with cement and turned into a patio behind the house. Mom and Dad laboriously mixed batch after batch in a wheelbarrow while, armed with spoons and sifters, I spent hours making mud pies and getting thoroughly coated with dirt. Engrossed in my task of sifting, I never noticed the big fuel truck backing up in the driveway. The huge tanker arrived once a year in the fall and deposited a thousand gallons of fuel oil for the winter.

Backing up a vehicle that size takes a special skill set, and the drivers can't see everything behind them. Certainly this driver didn't see me, a tiny girl camouflaged by a liberal layer of sand, playing in his path. The dogs saw him. Barking furiously they ran toward the truck, crowding and biting the wheels in an attempt to herd the danger away. The truck kept moving toward me. The dogs held their ground, refusing to move as the tires rubbed their sides and began dragging them down to be crushed.

The driver might not have seen me, but there was no missing four very large, noisy German shepherds. He stopped

23

the truck and, with a foolish level of bravery, attempted to step out and shoo the dogs away. He was a target they could sink their teeth into. If he'd been a split second slower slamming the cab door, they'd have been successful. The brief moment outside the truck allowed him to see just what the dogs guarded. He leaned on the truck horn until my parents came running to collect me and the dogs.

The dogs hated the big yellow school bus. It came with alarming regularity, swallowed up their children, and disappeared for hours. Thankfully, it returned us unharmed each afternoon. It required a significant amount of sniffing of clothes, faces, and hair to be sure. After several minutes, the afternoon blockade of furry bodies would release us to play.

Virginia had getting out the door without a dog in attendance down to a science. But I was a little kindergartner, outweighed by all of my fur-coated guardians, and I had more trouble.

We were running late one day and the bus driver blew the horn, warning us to hurry. My sister grabbed her lunch bag. "I'll go hold the bus, you hurry up."

She dashed out the door. I swung the heavy wooden portal shut. Sig got her nose in the way, preventing it from closing tightly, but it slowed her enough for me to slam the screen door. I took off at a run and leaped aboard only to feel the brush of barreling, fur-coated bodies slide past and block my path. Sig stopped and leaned, gently forcing me to retreat. I could see Electra applying the same tactics to my sister while Signet went to work on the child in the seat farthest back.

I turned to Mr. Galloway, the driver, for help. After all, Mom and Dad could always make the dogs obey. He sat statue-still, sweat streaming down his face and with an expression that made me think he had a stomachache. Mounty sat at his elbow, a deep rumbling growl rolling up from his chest. If Mr. Galloway moved, Mounty's lips curled back, exposing his rather ominous, ivory grin.

When in doubt, ask big sister. "What do we do?"

"I guess we get off," Virginia said. "The dogs always follow us."

I turned and swiftly hopped down the steps, my sister close behind. The dogs stayed on the bus. Mounty's growls got louder.

Virginia pointed toward the house. "Go get Mom and Dad."

One of our parents must have noticed the bus still sitting at the end of the driveway because they met me halfway. Dad climbed in and sternly ordered the dogs out. They ducked their heads, tucked back their ears, and looked up at him through their long spiky lashes, but they didn't move. He ran his fingers through his hair and watched in silence.

Thankfully Mounty had stopped growling, but Mr. Galloway didn't move unless you counted the beads of perspiration making salt trails on his face. Dad noticed the female dogs leaning on the children the way they leaned to steer my sister and me away from anything they considered dangerous.

"Okay, kids, the dogs think you're in danger and they want you off the bus. Can you please stand up and step outside?"

Farm kids take things in stride, and being hijacked and made late to school by a pack of dogs entertained the group. Swiftly, everyone climbed down the stairs and out into the morning sunshine. Signet, Electra, and Sig brought up the rear and watched for stragglers. Once off they circled the group of children, keeping everyone together. Mounty was the last to leave. He gave one last look at Mr. Galloway, licked his chops, and pranced down the steps. Mr. Galloway almost closed the door on the dog's tail.

Everyone had to walk to the house before we could get the dogs inside and convince the bus driver he could safely open the door and load up his passengers again. Years later when my sister had graduated and I was in seventh grade, the bus doors remained tightly closed whenever a dog was in sight.

One thing the dogs couldn't protect me from was germs. I had a bad bout of pneumonia at the age of four, and that's when my parents made the house rule that a shepherd had to sleep in my room.

Heat radiated off my skin in waves, and I struggled to kick off the warm cover surrounding me. Eyes closed, I rubbed the satin binding of the blanket. The softness usually helped me sleep. My lungs burned like I had run a really long way on a hot summer day. I was too tired to open my eyes. It didn't matter. Dad held and rocked me, his soft, deep voice a thread of safety holding back the hurt. I opened my eyes a crack, but light from the rising sun made me squish them closed. Mounty licked the toes I'd managed to squirm beyond a fold in the blanket.

"How is she?" Mom asked.

"About the same. If the fever doesn't break by tonight, we're going to have to take her to the hospital."

"How are we going to pay the bill? It took us years to pay off the last time she was there with pneumonia."

"We'll find a way. We really don't have a choice, do we?"

I could hear the sound of Mom's dress rubbing against her slip. A wave of her perfume enveloped me and then I felt her lips brush my cheek.

Dad sighed and shifted in the rocker. "You better go to work. They're not going to let you have any more time off, and we may need the money. I'll call in today."

The steady rhythm of the rocker returned. It made it easier to breathe.

"The roads are icy," he said. "Take your time."

Mom's perfume faded. The kitchen door closed in the distance. Silence except for the creak of the rocker. Sleep.

"Hey, sweetie. Take a sip of this."

I opened my eyes. The setting sun turned the room shades of orange, but with more red than the juice in the glass Dad held to my lips. The cold, acid taste cut through the cottony tin flavor in my mouth. It burned my sore throat and exploded in my stomach. I sat up coughing and fought the urge to return the juice. Then the other coughing started. Deep in my chest, I couldn't stop it. I couldn't breathe but still I coughed. Dad shifted me to his shoulder and paced the room, gently patting my back and murmuring words I didn't have the energy to understand.

Gradually the coughing stopped. Dad continued to pace across the room, back and forth. I could hear Mounty's nails clicking on the tile floor. He walked beside Dad, step for step, turn and walk. His nose found my foot again and licked.

"Tell me about Sig and the stranger." My voice sounded different but I knew I'd spoken the words.

"You were there, and it was only a few months ago." Dad's voice rumbled under my ear.

"Tell me."

Dad sighed, but it was the smile kind of sigh. "The dogs are your guardians. They won't let anyone near you. They know their job is to keep you safe, and they don't trust any grown-ups but Mom and me."

Dad shifted me to his other shoulder. "A strange man came to the house and tried to give you candy. Mounty pushed you out of the way and barked and growled and snarled until the man was backed up against the retaining wall. The wall was taller than the man, and Mounty had his attention. He didn't see Sig running along the top of the wall ready to pounce down on him. He would have been in big trouble if I hadn't called her."

The story made me giggle, like always. I could hear Mounty—click, click, click—as his nails tapped the floor with each step. A dog was near, I was safe. Shivers claimed me and I snuggled inside the blanket. Dad returned to the rocker and I heard Mounty thump to the floor and sigh. My eyes drifted shut. It still hurt to breathe, but sleep came.

"How is she?" A wave of perfume touched my nose.

"Better, the fever's down and she's been sleeping most of the day."

"You must be exhausted. With the door closed, her room is the warmest in the house and no drafts. Let's put her to bed and get some sleep. It's been a long three days and we're both going to have to go to work tomorrow or we'll lose our jobs."

"If she's better, maybe it'll be okay to leave her with her sister."

I felt myself being carried up the stairs and tucked into bed. Mounty stayed beside my bed on the floor. I heard the door close and drifted back to sleep.

28

My skin was on fire. I hurt so badly and I couldn't breathe. My lungs burned and I felt my arms thrash and my body jerk. A cold nose poked my back, a paw held me in place, and a tongue licked my face. What was wrong with Mounty? His tongue was never cold. The paw and the nose disappeared and I fought for more air. Vaguely I knew a loud banging kept happening, like someone throwing a boulder against the door to my room. Wood shattered. Cool air washed my skin, blessed relief. Mom's hand pressed against my forehead. Had she been outside? Her hand was so cold.

"Bob, come quick! The fever's back. She's going into convulsions."

I don't remember what happened after that.

The sun crept through my bedroom window. I opened my eyes to a big black nose and sad German shepherd eyes. "Is Mounty okay? His tongue was cold."

Dad pulled the blanket up and tucked it under my chin. His hand gave Mounty a quick pat as he withdrew it. "He's fine. He's probably bruised from breaking down your door, but he doesn't seem to notice."

"He broke down my door?"

"He realized you were really sick and needed your mom and me. He broke down your bedroom door to come get us. He saved your life."

"That's what German shepherds do, Dad," I said. "They protect their kids."

29

When Scooter Met Scott

Max Parks

The rules were straightforward but extremely difficult to obey. My orders were to ask no questions, offer no opinions, make no suggestions, and impart no information. I could respond precisely to narrowly tailored questions, but only if specifically asked to do so. If my response was deemed "off subject" or in any way deficient, the phone call was abruptly terminated. If the call ended badly, and it sometimes did, I might not get another call for months.

The rules were crafted by my son Scott, who suffered from one of the most devastating forms of mental illness—paranoid schizophrenia. It is every bit as bad as it sounds. His mother and I had watched helplessly as the condition slowly took over Scott's mind, transforming him from a successful student and college athlete into a haggard recluse who retreated into a darkened apartment in a bad part of town. He came out only at night once or twice a month to buy groceries at a twenty-four-hour store. He had not been to a laundromat or barber in years. He refused medication. And there was absolutely nothing we could do to help. He would not pick up the phone, read our letters, or answer a knock at the door. If we hadn't paid his rent, he would have been homeless. Or worse.

Our only connection was the occasional phone call, and to keep that tenuous link alive, I usually did my best to follow the rules. I figured that if he was talking to me at all, even if the call came with a dozen baffling rules, it showed that he wanted some kind of contact with me. I took a small shred of hope in that fact. But there was so much I wanted to say, so much I needed to say. I longed for a way to give him his life back, and I knew I had to somehow move him beyond the strict confines of the phone and his rambling monologues. I needed to see him again. So one day I took a chance and broke a rule.

"I'd like you to meet our new dog."

Silence.

The seconds clicked slowly by. I braced myself, waiting for the line to go dead.

"You are never supposed to ask me anything or give me information I don't ask for," he said.

"I know. I'm sorry. I just really want you to meet Scooter. I think you would like him. He loves to fetch."

Long pause.

"What happened to Buck?" Scott asked.

Buck was the abandoned dog Scott had brought home fourteen years earlier. That lovable and loyal old mutt had been part of our family most of Scott's life.

"He died a year ago," I replied.

There was another long, very long, pause before he spoke.

31

"You could have told me."

"It wasn't on the list of things you said I can do," I said softly.

"True."

Long pause.

"Want to meet Scooter?"

Silence.

I knew I was pushing the limits. But simply getting this far had been a staggering success. More seconds clicked by.

"How did Buck die?"

"He just wore out with age, Scott. He had lost his sight and most of his hearing. One day he couldn't eat or drink, so we had the vet put him to sleep. They made it painless."

"He was a good dog. I am going to go now. I will call you later," Scott said.

"Okay. When do you think you will call?"

Click.

I had broken too many rules for one day.

But Scott called a week later. He began to launch into another one-sided speech about a scientific theory I could not understand, and I broke a very major rule and interrupted him.

"Scooter wants to meet you."

Pause.

"No, he doesn't. He doesn't know I exist. You are using him as a means to persuade me to come over."

"Is it working?" I asked.

He did not hang up, and I may have even heard a laugh. *Please God, keep him on the line.*

"If I came over, your dog might attack me," Scott said.

"No, he wouldn't. He loves people. He is always happy to meet new people," I replied.

"He would sense that you fear me."

"I don't fear you," I replied, lying through my teeth.

The truth is that my wife and I feared what Scott's condition could lead to. There were indications that someone had tried to break into our home on more than one occasion, and one night when I could not sleep I saw Scott's car parked in front of our home at 3:00 a.m. Yes, I feared him. But I also deeply loved him. That is the tension and dilemma of a parent who has a mentally ill child.

"Your dog would sense your anxiety. Dogs are pack animals. He would try to defend you as the pack leader."

We are still talking! Thank you, God!

Scott negotiated elaborate terms and conditions but agreed to come over. The meeting would happen after dark. No one could be in the house but me. Scooter would have to be in the backyard and could watch our interaction through the sliding glass door. If the dog seemed hostile, Scott would leave.

We had a deal!

We set the date. And then my wife and I prayed. Hard.

On the agreed day, the knock came. Scott was two hours late, but there he was. The Red Sea had actually parted, manna had fallen from heaven, and I was walking on water.

His hair was far too long and way too greasy, and his unkempt beard made him look like a wild man, but it was a beautiful sight to see him on the front porch.

Although Scooter is an extremely friendly dog, Scott's words had been haunting me. What if my dog perceived the tension? What if he smelled fear? What if he could tell my heart was hammering the walls of my chest? One bark and it would be over.

Scott stepped into the living room and found Scooter on the alert, staring at him through the glass.

"I'll hold his collar while I let him in, and then I'll bring him slowly over to you," I told Scott.

"Okay. But hold him tight."

I slid the door open, reached down for Scooter's collar, and clutched air as my dog bolted past me at the speed of a bullet. I gasped, powerless to control whatever happened next.

Scooter is a good-sized hunting dog, and he was barreling toward Scott as fast as four legs can move a canine. Scott stepped back into a corner by the front door and found himself trapped by the happiest dog on earth. Scooter's tail banged the wall with uncontained joy at meeting my son.

If my dog had sensed any of my fear, it must have been drowned out by the more intense sense of love.

Scott petted Scooter's head, then his back, and soon we were all outside playing fetch.

It was one of the best days of my life.

Scooter made sure we had no time to talk of awkward things, of lost years, of missed Christmases. He wanted to play. Again and again and again. So we laughed, and chased, and threw the ball until Scott felt the need to leave.

But we made plans for another visit, and Scott kept the date.

The dam had broken. The earth had moved. We were in a new world, and Scooter was making it safe for both father and son. The dog was the diplomat. As my son and my dog played for hours in the backyard, Scooter asked no questions, offered no opinions, made no suggestions, and imparted no information. And that is what Scott needed at that point in his life.

That was two years ago. A lot has happened since then, some good, some terrible, and much great. Scott was eventually hospitalized by order of the court and given medication against his will. Slowly but surely he emerged from the fog of his madness.

Today he is again in college, making up for lost time, pulling straight As, celebrating every holiday with us, and having dinner with us most weekends. Scott hugs his mom again, goes to church again, rides a bike in broad daylight again, goes out to dinner with friends, travels—and plays with Scooter regularly.

They say that God works in mysterious ways. I firmly believe that God used the love of a dog to help begin the process of pulling Scott out of his mental illness and reconnecting our family. And I am deeply, deeply grateful.

Willie Nelson and the Open Tread Stairs

Millie Martin

Our daughter, Shelley, laughs when she recalls seeing her golden retriever, Willie, for the first time. She and her husband, Erik Nelson, made choosing the family pet one of the first major decisions as newlyweds. They researched breeds. Shelley favored a lapdog. Erik wanted a *man's* dog. Erik won. They decided on a golden retriever and selected a reputable breeder nearby. They had the pick of the litter. Since Erik picked the breed, he wanted Shelley to make the final choice.

She didn't hesitate. The affable puppy that plopped in the middle of the feeding bowl captured her heart. It was a definite indication of Willie's love of food—a trait that became the reason for our constant vigilance when he grew to a larger-than-average golden height and filled out a ninety-pound frame. His nose stood at kitchen counter level and food left unattended was fair game. He once devoured the corner of a shower cake. Quick thinking and a bouquet of fresh flowers concealed the missing piece before guests arrived.

Shelley and Erik bestowed the Nelson family name on Willie and showered him with attention. He wore a bandana around his neck, mimicking the ever-present headband of his namesake, and howled to "Whiskey River" and other Willie Nelson hits. Their Willie adorned their Christmas cards. They planned doggie playdates for him. He accompanied Erik on morning runs. When Erik traveled, as he frequently did, Willie was a companion and source of comfort for Shelley. He made her feel more secure. While his size made him appear formidable, we knew that inside he was a cream puff—information we hoped an intruder wouldn't guess.

We often kept our grand-doggie, especially after he pined away during one brief boarding experience. At his doggie grandparents' house, the gentle giant cowered at his reflection in the glass door. He barked, then ran at seeing his own image in the swimming pool. However, it was the open tread stairs at our home that sparked Willie's greatest fear.

Though always at Shelley's heels, when the Nelsons visited our house, Willie wouldn't follow Shelley to the upstairs bedroom. He balked at the sight of the open tread stairs, refusing to go up. On the Nelson visits, my husband and I knew Willie would sleep downstairs in our bedroom.

Shelley and Erik celebrated their first anniversary and then a second. We tried not to ask when we would have a grandbaby with fingers and toes rather than paws. We hoped that would come in time. In secret, we speculated about Willie's reaction at an addition to the Nelson family—a baby who cried and demanded attention.

Shortly after their second wedding anniversary, Shelley and Erik came for a visit and shared the joyful news of their first pregnancy. We were elated but eager for an outward change in Shelley's appearance, a little baby bump, to make the event seem real.

On the evening of this visit and just after the blissful announcement, we placed Willie's bed downstairs in our room as usual. To our surprise, without hesitation, Willie followed Shelley up the dreaded steps. He needed no visible evidence of her condition. He had an uncanny sense of her pregnancy and his protectiveness overcame his fear. He traipsed up the open tread stairs and took up his vigil beside her bed, a practice he continued until our initial joy turned to sorrow with the loss of the tiny life that had just begun.

Willie sensed the loss and clung even closer to Shelley. When her second pregnancy also ended in a miscarriage, Willie comforted her in the despondency she hid from even those closest to her. The only time he was far from her side was during her visits to our home, where his original fear of the open treads once again kept him from following her upstairs. He would settle instead in his bed in our room downstairs.

When Shelley shared the news of her third pregnancy, we all held the information close and decided to tell no one until Shelley was safely into her third month and would no longer be able to conceal the news. While we decided not to breathe a word, not even to close friends and family, Willie knew. On their visit to our home, he ignored his usual spot in our bedroom and followed Shelley up the horrid stairs. Then our granddaughter arrived, followed in two years by her brother, and Willie continued his pattern. During Shelley's pregnancies, he followed her upstairs and slept by her bed. After the safe arrival of each child, he resumed sleeping downstairs in our bedroom during their visits and warily stayed clear of the stairs.

Two small preschoolers kept the Nelson household busy. Willie may have puzzled about the change in his position, from being on the front of Christmas cards to now hoping he was fed, but he remained gentle and patient. The morning runs with Erik became less frequent, and trips to the groomer were traded for a bath and a quick brushing, but Willie didn't seem to mind. He welcomed the additional love and most likely never missed the doggie playdates. He became the preschoolers' playmate, their pillow, and their friend.

With a four-year-old and two-year-old, most assumed the Nelson family had a "quiver full." Certainly when they arrived at our house, their SUV was overflowing with Willie, two children, and all the accompanying paraphernalia.

One particular visit caught us by surprise. While always excited to see each of the Nelsons, it seemed odd to have a return visit so soon. We didn't question the reason.

Just before bedtime, they told us their joyful news, the real purpose of the visit. Again, we agreed to keep the announcement secret for just a bit longer, but to a watchful eye there was one visible sign, one outward indication that a third grandchild was on the way. It was Willie—Willie at Shelley's heels when she went upstairs for bed, Willie making his brave ascent up the open tread stairs, ready to stand guard at her bedside.

On the Train to London

Andrea Doering

I didn't know I needed a dog that day. But God did.

I was twelve years old, and my mother decided to take my older sister and me on a trip to England and Scotland. We appeared to be in the middle of redefining our family. My father and mother had separated a few months before. I went to school, I went to swim practice, I talked to my friends. But I was shutting down, kind of circling the wagons around myself. On the outside nothing suffered, but inside I was suffering the aftershocks of my own earthquake. I loved my dad, I loved our family life—why anyone would want to leave that I could not fathom. It made me wonder if my understanding of life and people was completely off-kilter. Added to that were the first waves of adolescence. For someone who did not like change, these were miserable times.

So we were on a train the spring I turned twelve, on our way back to England from a few days in Scotland. We'd forgotten to reserve a sleeper—these things happened when traveling with my carefree mother—so we'd settled into one of the coach cars for a long night. This was one of those old-fashioned ones you see in the movies, with tweedy cushioned seats that face each other, racks overhead, and a sliding door to the corridor.

Just as the train was getting ready to pull out of the station that night, a middle-aged gentleman opened our compartment door and joined us, bringing with him what looked like a large black wolf. The man nodded at us, placed his very British-looking wool hat on the rack above, and told his companion to sit.

Those days it took a lot for me to look beyond my own circumstances, but the presence of this large black dog succeeded. I was fascinated. He was the most regal looking animal I'd ever been close to, and there he sat—on his own seat, reserved and paid for—with a calm expression that looked for all the world like a prince granting an audience to his subjects.

His owner was happy to tell us more about him. This amazing black creature turned out to be a Belgian shepherd. I'd never even heard of that kind of dog—and in truth he was lovelier than any wolf. Thick, jet black fur stood out like a husky, not a shepherd. He was about three feet tall at his head, and a magnificent head it was too—alert, full of interest and patience. I'd never seen an animal this beautiful.

He continued to sit in his seat, but as soon as his owner

gave the word, he jumped down and crossed the compartment to me, allowing me the privilege of petting his head. There was no other way to describe his look. I must have done something right, because for the rest of our long night ride to London, he sat not on his own seat but with me in mine. And while I sat there with a great black blanket of fur, something inside me began to open up again. Those parts of me that didn't want to love, didn't want to be hurt again, began a slow fade into the background. If this amazing animal saw worth in me, I couldn't be all wrong in my view of the world. I could find ways to share myself with others, much as he had done with me.

At that time we didn't have a dog. My mother must have sensed that this could be a key to our moving on, and when we returned home, she sought and found Zachary—a Belgian shepherd as wise and beautiful and loving as the one who befriended me on the train. During the months my father lived apart from us, Zachary kept me from shutting down. And when my father returned, Zachary was a bridge to finding ways to trust Dad again, as the two of us took my dog on long walks together, enjoying his calm, regal look at the world. That same acceptance I'd experienced on the train was present in Zachary too—and it gave me the confidence to trust others, and to trust that though the future would bring change, it would be filled with love.

The Purpose-Driven Dog

C.J. Darlington

She wasn't much to look at. Scruffy yellow fur, bent ears sticking straight out from the sides of her head. A conglomerate of Lab, golden retriever, and terrier. Just another unwanted mutt at the animal shelter.

Mom still doesn't know why she took my sister and me to the pound that day. I don't remember much, since I was only four years old, but I do have a hazy memory of spotting the dog in a cage smelling of disinfectant. She was plaintively whimpering and clawing at the chain link, like she was trying to reach us. Mom couldn't resist, and the dog came home with us right then and there.

We named her Cindy after pop singer Cyndi Lauper (it was the 80s after all), and she got along well with our dalmatian, Sparky. But Cindy had a destructive gene and a strange aversion to stuffed animals, which was a big problem because my sister and I owned and loved many of them. It wasn't as if Cindy shredded the toys into small pieces. She would meticulously rip off only their faces and leave the mutilated carcasses for us to find later. This frustrated my parents to no end. More than once my sister and I would receive a brand-new, expensive stuffed animal for our birthday or Christmas, and the next day we'd find a faceless plush corpse.

Cindy belonged to our family, but she and I had a special bond. Without fail, every time I'd try to run across the yard Cindy would tackle me, taking me down with a hook of her paw. If I ran through the house it was the same thing. I'd get frustrated with her, but it made me feel like Cindy was mine. She never wrestled with anyone but me.

A few years later we moved to another place. I got a little bigger and harder to trip. Our home was a good one for a dog, but in some ways Cindy never fit in. She didn't have any tricks like Sparky. She wasn't beautiful like the shepherd mix who joined our family later. She was just Cindy.

"What a useless dog," my dad joked one day as he took a home video of the family and zoomed in on Cindy. He didn't say it to be mean, but I never liked hearing those words. We wouldn't dare talk about the humans in our family that way; why could we talk like that about our dog? About *my* dog.

When I was eight we found out my grandfather had cancer. The doctors discovered it too late to do anything, and by that time it had spread throughout his body. He didn't have long to live. At my age, death was a foreign thing. I knew Grandpappy was sick, but even when my mom told me he'd died in the hospital, the news went over my head.

The news that came later didn't.

I don't remember the exact way my parents suggested giving Cindy to my grandmother, but I remember the devastation of my young heart. They gently explained how Grammy was all alone in her big house. Having a dog would be just the thing for her, and the fact that Cindy was already trained and not a puppy made even more sense.

They left the final decision to me. I cried at the thought of not having Cindy anymore, but inside I knew they were right. Grammy needed *my* dog. And it wasn't like she'd be gone. We could visit her down in Virginia whenever we wanted.

It turned out the transition wasn't as hard as I thought it would be, for me or for Cindy. The next five years were some of the best of Cindy's life. My grandmother doted on her like she was her only child. She lavished her with toys, beds, and treats. I'd imagine Grammy lying in bed at night, feeling safe with Cindy by her side. "What a good dog," she'd whisper as she drifted off to sleep.

Whenever we could, we drove the three and a half hours for visits, and Grammy swore Cindy knew when we were coming.

Maybe she heard Grammy talking to Mom on the phone, or maybe there was some unknown signal Grammy was sending. But it was uncanny the way Cindy would become restless in the hours before we'd arrive, and because of that Grammy nicknamed her Cindy the Wonder Dog.

My grandmother's house had a bay window in front, and when we'd pull up in the driveway, Cindy's head would instantly pop up in that window. If she happened to be outside when we arrived, she'd cry and carry on when she saw our car. We'd have fun trying to sneak up on her, but it never worked.

Every Christmas Grammy would come up to our home in Pennsylvania. I remember watching her in the driveway, and it was hilarious to see my grandmother trying to balance Christmas gifts in one arm while being yanked to the front door by tail-wagging, gleeful Cindy.

Hang Loose!

His name was Sandy, and he lived at Waikiki Beach where he was friends with all the other Hawaiian surfers of his time. He rode that surfboard every day. He loved the big waves, and if they weren't grand enough, he'd abandon the fun and swim back to shore, where restaurateurs were always thrilled to see him arrive. He became known all over the nation for his unusual surfing skill. When he died, he was given a proper surfer's funeral, his ashes taken out to sea by his friends in a huge flotilla of canoes.

Oh yes . . . and he was a dog.

Sandy the Surfing Dog became legendary on Waikiki Beach during the 1950s. A local "poi dog" (or a mongrel stray), he actually achieved fame for his love of the breakers, and his picture riding a surfboard appeared in newspapers around the country. When he died of natural causes, the surfers of Waikiki gave him the kind of ceremonial send-off they always gave one of their own.[4]

I don't know if Grammy ever wondered how she would go on without my grandfather, but I do know that having Cindy gave her a reason to come home. Cindy needed her. If there was ever a chance of thunderstorms, Grammy would cancel her plans and stay home with Cindy, who was scared of storms. If Cindy so much as lifted her paw oddly, Grammy would rush her to the vet to check it out. She talked to Cindy constantly—not in puppy talk but in a normal voice, as if to a friend.

Grammy died when I was thirteen, and there was never a question where Cindy would go. She came full circle back to where she started. She was a little grayer around the muzzle, but she hadn't lost her spunk and could still chase sticks and tug toys for hours.

One sunny fall day, I ran outside on the deck to where Cindy was waiting. Just like when we were both younger, her paw hooked around my leg and she did her best to trip me. I laughed, shaking my head, but I didn't go down. We'd all come to realize this useless dog wasn't useless after all. Cindy had a purpose beyond what we could have ever imagined standing in the noisy shelter that day.

The Dog Next Door

Richard Meserva

My wife, Dawn, and I had a dog named Bo, a border collie mix we got as a puppy. He was rescued from the side of a highway when he was just a little guy, and he was my best buddy for many years. And he was a big part of this story.

Bo was an alpha dog in every way, with no patience for other dogs. He had a great personality but could be very intimidating. Neighborhood dogs that roamed free in our development never set foot on our—well, Bo's property. They could sit at the edge but go no farther.

The only dog Bo ever tolerated was Rex, the dog who lived next door. A purebred border collie himself, Rex was not allowed to roam even in his backyard. He stayed in a pen that measured around twelve by eighteen feet. It was attached to the house with a pet door leading inside, and that's all the territory he had. So there he would sit in his cage.

Rex's owner, Mrs. Carter, was elderly and didn't get around well. I also think maybe she didn't understand that a border collie needs a job or at the very least lots of exercise. Rex didn't have that at all. The only exercise he got was roaming inside the small ranch house and hanging out in the pen outdoors.

I know Mrs. Carter loved Rex, and she took good care of him in other ways, or at least she believed she did. She'd gotten him as a puppy and had him trained right away, so he was very obedient. But she soon became too feeble to exercise him. She also overfed him, in particular with table scraps. So Rex became something you seldom see—a fat border collie.

49

During the day, Rex would sit outside in his pen and stare at our house with his pale eyes. And for some reason, Bo seemed to take a liking to this caged dog. I would often find Bo hunkered down on the grass right next to Rex's fence with Rex sitting on the other side of the fence. The two dogs sometimes paced back and forth side by side, in step with one another, the chain-link fence between them. Dawn believed that Bo somehow understood what the other dog was going through and that he would sit or walk with him out of empathy. Bo would not deal with any other dog at all. Only Rex.

I owned a gym until a few years ago, and Bo would go with me to work. One afternoon Dawn called me at the gym to tell me that there might be a problem next door. By now Mrs. Carter was in her nineties. Her husband had died, and she lived alone with Rex. Dawn noticed the dog hadn't been outside in awhile. Now the postal carrier told her that Mrs. Carter's mail was piling up, and nobody was answering next door. Obviously something was wrong.

I called to Bo to come with me and drove home right away. I parked my truck, got out, and circled Mrs. Carter's house to see if I could possibly find a way to get inside without breaking in. I looked in her bedroom window, and in my limited line of vision I could see her legs on the bed, not moving. I got a stepladder to see better, and then it was clear to me that Mrs. Carter was dead. Her bedside lamp was tipped over her body, and Rex was lying on the floor next to her bed. Dawn called the police.

After Mrs. Carter had been taken away, the police talked to me. It appeared that she had died in her sleep of natural causes about three days before. Rex apparently would not leave her. He was all right but had not eaten in that time. His waste was all over the bedroom, and when the police entered the room, Rex still lay next to his owner's bed.

The police told me it was too late in the day to call animal control, so they planned to leave Rex in the house overnight and come back the next day for him. I'm sure they meant well, but I couldn't believe this. The dog was traumatized already, and to leave him there with the smell of death would be cruel. So Dawn and I offered to take Rex for now, which the police agreed to as long as we left a note on the door alerting any next of kin as to where Rex was.

We took Rex home that night. Once he was outside his fence and on Bo's territory, I worried that Bo would be aggressive with him like he was with other dogs. But that didn't happen. The two dogs were still buddies.

So Rex stayed with us. It was a few months before we heard from any next of kin, and of course we had fallen in love with the dog during that time. Mrs. Carter's son eventually showed up at our house. He was elderly himself and living in another state. He loved dogs but had his own, so he was greatly relieved when we asked to keep Rex.

Now Rex had a new life with Bo and with us. Dawn had always been a cat lover, but she and Rex bonded, and he went everywhere with her. Dawn had a hair salon right next door to our gym, so every day I took Bo to work with me in my truck, and Dawn took Rex to work with her in her car. Rex had gone through losing Mr. Carter, then Mrs. Carter, and now in his anxiety he shadowed Dawn constantly, herding her and obsessively moving when he was indoors with her.

Rex was well-trained, and at first we didn't understand just how well. We didn't know until Mrs. Carter's son showed up why Rex wouldn't budge sometimes—he had been trained not to move from place to place outdoors without a leash. Until we discovered that, we had to bodily pick him up to put him inside or outside a vehicle. Sometimes Dawn would literally push the poor dog out of her car to get him moving.

One of Rex's many quirks was that he was afraid of linoleum. I never knew why, but he would not walk on it. So we arranged the traffic rugs at both the hair salon and the gym to accommodate nervous Rex and his linoleum phobia. He was worth the trouble.

I'm an outdoors guy, and I took Rex out walking and eventually running with Bo and me. With exercise and proper dog food, Rex slimmed right down. The two dogs became running buddies, chasing each other, teasing over toys. The communication between them was amazing. It was as if Bo had somehow rescued Rex after all those years of visiting through the fence, and Rex knew it.

I'm happy to report that Rex lived to be old and his last several years with us were good ones. When the day came that he needed to be put down, we took him to our vet, who was a great guy. He squatted down, opened his arms, and said, "Come here, Rex."

Rex walked right into the vet's arms—straight across a linoleum floor.

Rescue on Round Top Mountain

Sandy Cathcart

When I was nine years old, traveling with my father in the dark of night over the back roads of Northern California, I had my first encounter with a mountain lion. Its fur was as black as the inside of an abandoned well. Dad called it a panther. But there were no panthers in the area of the Trinity Alps, or so we were told.

This animal was about the size of a full-grown man. It fell off the side of the mountain and landed right in front of our truck. My dog and best friend, Nipper, went wild, barking and lunging at the windshield. Dad stopped our old pickup just in time to avoid running into the lion.

"Stay in the truck, Sandra," he said.

He didn't have to say *that* twice.

With Nipper barking frantically in my ear, I watched as Dad squeezed out of the truck, closed the door with a snap, and walked over toward the crumpled black form, easily visible in the light cast by our headlights.

Panther. Just the sound of the word on my tongue conjured up horrifying stories in my mind of young children being dragged from their beds into the jungle. It didn't take much imagination to envision the panther grabbing Dad and dragging him into the thick forest, leaving Nipper and me alone. I wasn't sure which would be worse—to see Dad taken off by a crazed panther, or to be left alone to face Bigfoot.

Because I was sure that someday Bigfoot *would* come, and Nipper would be no match for him. Nipper was a huge German shepherd and wolf mix, more silver than black, with long legs and light eyes that could bore into your soul. But I figured even Nipper would have problems with Bigfoot.

Dad had just passed the left headlight, causing a big shadow to spread across the road, when the panther sprang to its feet and took off over the side of the mountain. I never saw Dad move so fast. He was around the truck and back in the driver's seat before the panther's tail had disappeared into the darkness. Nipper jumped in my lap, pawing at the passenger window and barking madly.

Dad and I talked of little else for days. Everyone thought we were crazy.

"There are no panthers in our woods!" neighbors kept insisting.

But it was hard for them to argue when Dad pointed to me as an eyewitness. I reveled in my high standing for as long as I could. It wasn't often I received my father's praise.

I was raised an only child, and the three years we spent on a thousand-acre ranch in Northern California were my happiest. Back when I was seven, Dad had given me a snakebite kit and taught me to tell time and direction by the sun. After he and Mama were convinced of my wilderness survival skills, they let me roam through the forest as carefree and fearless as any wild animal. I wasn't afraid. After all, I was more at home with animals than I was with people, and I had Nipper to watch out for me, unless he was off chasing something else, which was about half the time. Being part wolf meant he had a lot of things to chase.

I loved burying my face in Nipper's fur. He loved it too. He would lean into me until we were both leaning so hard that if either one of us moved, we would both fall. He kept me warm on days when the wind blew cold from the north, and he never tired of playing our favorite game where I would put on an old pair of jeans and run until he caught my leg and pulled me to the ground. Then off we'd go again. His teeth never broke my skin though they shredded many pairs of jeans.

Perhaps it was because he was part wolf, or perhaps it was because of his enormous size; whatever the reason, most people were afraid of Nipper. Most of the time that was a good thing, because his presence gave me protection. His bark would alert me to a rattlesnake in my path or scare away a bobcat or bear.

One day when I was about eight, both my parents were busy with company—distant relatives I'd never seen before. I decided to head out to the woods, and I decided to leave Nipper behind. Being convinced wild animals understood me, I had it in my child's mind to find a bear and strike up some kind of conversation. If Nipper came with me, he would chase the bear before I would have a chance to talk.

I heel-toed it through the forest up Round Top Mountain, just like my father taught me, being careful not to step on a twig or crunchy leaves. You had to be quiet to sneak up on a bear. After awhile, instead of finding a bear, I saw a strange man. He was sneaking through the trees. I didn't recognize him, but I assumed he was one of the distant relatives. It looked as if he was following my trail.

"Where are you, girlie?" he called.

He was using a soft voice as if he was playing a game of hide-and-seek.

Before I could answer, Nipper suddenly appeared at my feet in that quiet way of his that was so much like a wolf. He whimpered quietly as his light eyes darted from the man to me.

"Girlie . . ." the man called again.

Nipper whimpered again and started away, not on the usual path home, which would have taken us closer to the man, but farther into the woods where I had never been before. He looked back at me. He clearly wanted me to follow him.

"Little girlie . . ."

The man was closer. I could see his shape through the brush, but he hadn't spotted me. I wasn't sure what to do. The sun was getting lower in the sky. If I followed Nipper into the forest, I might get stuck out here overnight. Though I didn't fear finding a bear in the daylight, I sure didn't want to bump into one at night, and I couldn't help thinking of that panther. Imagine running into something like that!

The man was hacking his way through the brush now, getting closer. Since I didn't know who he was, I didn't necessarily have reason to be afraid of him, except for the fact Nipper didn't like him. I made the decision to trust the instincts of my dog.

I followed as Nipper led me deeper into the darkened forest. I tried to be as quiet as I could, but several times my foot made a twig snap. It seemed to echo through the forest like the falling of a tree limb. The crashing of the man's steps was even louder. He was farther away, but still coming.

Nipper kept leading me higher. When the sun sank low in the sky, I began to think about that panther. The thought almost made me turn around and take my chances with the man. How dangerous could a distant relative be?

It was as if Nipper read my thoughts. He came back and leaned into me. I sat down and buried my face in his fur, starting to cry. Instead of leaning back like he normally would, Nipper pulled away and whimpered again, so I got up and followed him. It wasn't long before we came to the edge of the forest. All the fear left me when I spotted our barn's roof two hillsides below. Sunlight bathed the entire scene.

I started skipping across the field, happy that I would be home in a few minutes.

Suddenly I heard running footsteps behind me. The man wasn't calling my name anymore, but he was looking straight at me and he was moving fast! His eyes reminded me of the panther.

Pumping my arms and legs, I ran.

Nipper turned and chased the man, biting his legs like he did in our chasing games. Judging by the man's yelps, Nipper must have been sinking his teeth into skin.

Dad suddenly appeared around the corner of the barn. When he looked up the hill, his face turned into an angry storm. At first I thought he was mad at me. I had never seen a look like that on his face before. I froze as he ran past me and after the man.

My dad was strong and fast. He always won the arm wrestling contests against my uncles. He was yelling at the man.

I had to turn away when he started beating the man with his fists.

Nipper came to my side, and I buried my face in his fur. This time he leaned back into me.

It wasn't until I was much older that I heard the words "child molester," and I realized that God had used my dog and childhood best friend to save me that day from a terrible fate. While it may not be true that dogs understand human language, you will never convince me they don't understand God talk. How else would Nipper have known to come rescue me like he did?

To this day, I am thankful that God used a dog not only to rescue me but also to meet the needs of a lonely child. I learned a lot about love and commitment from that relationship, enough to carry me through the rest of my life.

Coming Home

Sherri Gallagher

That Saturday was one of those perfect days. I loaded my Afghan hound, Yours Truly Raspberry Ice, into the truck, and we were off. I'm not sure which of us spent more time hanging our heads out the windows to enjoy the wind and smells. I love the fall. The air was so cool and crisp I could eat it like candy. The colors exploded around me, and everywhere I looked the picture kept changing.

I'm not sure how Raspberry got her name. I did find she had a penchant for raspberry ice cream, but her history was shrouded in a kaleidoscope of changing homes. She'd be purchased for her excellent bloodlines, fail miserably in the show ring, and be shuffled off to someone else.

All my dogs knew errands ended at the ice cream stand with a chocolate shake for me and a dish of ice cream for them. Well, all of them but Raspberry. I had purchased her a year earlier and was still trying to get her to bond to me. For two years she had bounced from show home to show home, changing every two to three months until she was afraid to trust. She'd look at me with those big brown eyes as if she were asking whether I would reject her too. Dogs don't necessarily understand words, so I struggled to find the actions to prove myself worthy. My other dogs had trusted immediately. I was theirs, and they could depend on me for all things from kibble to ice cream to cuddles. Raspberry ignored them with the aloofness bred into Afghan hounds.

Physically, she was a showstopper with an unusual reverse coloring called "domino." Her long silky hair gradually moved from black at her back through gray to white—picture perfect. But she would cringe in the show ring, greeting everyone with the physical actions of submission that made her a failure as a show dog.

My male Afghan, Khan, was day to Raspberry's night. Typical cream color, sporting a pink nose, crooked teeth, and a chest so narrow his front feet should have crossed, he'd walk into the ring with the regal elegance of a king allowing the peasants to gaze upon his beauty. His attitude put us in the ribbons even if we didn't deserve to be there. I'd started

showing him as a lark, a good excuse for my husband and me to get out of town for a weekend.

As time went on, I dreamed of establishing a small kennel. While I loved Khan, the purpose of breeding is to create improvement. Of course good breed stock is expensive, and as newlyweds with huge student loans hanging over our heads, we didn't have the finances.

I shared my secret dreams with a breeder friend. She thought for a while and then introduced me to Raspberry. She'd been at a show and Raspberry's owner had returned from the ring in a huff. The dog had known he was furious and had slunk into her crate. Softhearted Jill took one look and bought Raspberry on the spot. She vowed to find just the right home for this pretty little girl.

Raspberry had been raised in a home for autistic children. They would stroke her and hit her and she would love them. We were told some children would develop an attachment to her and come out of their internal world. But her life in the school had also left her never knowing if a person was going to pet her or swat her.

No one had been willing to take time with her until she came to me. Show dogs had to produce results and justify the expense of their existence or they were left behind like so much trash on the roadside of big dreams. But I did my best to shelter and nurture her. After a year, she still greeted me with the same level of friendliness she showed to a stranger walking down the street. It made me wonder whether it would matter to her if she never saw me again.

On this particular fall day, I found a nice grassy spot, set down her dish, looped the leash on my arm, and relaxed on a bench. A sharp jerk to my arm interrupted my reverie.

Raspberry was at the very end of her twelve-foot leash, head up, tail wagging, and focused on something in the distance. Her ice cream dish was turned upside down, her treat melting into the grass. Her eyes were riveted across the parking lot of the nearby shopping center.

She bounced two feet straight in the air, landing only to fly up again, so I gave in to her tugging and my curiosity. Raspberry did her best sled dog imitation across the pavement with me as the sled.

About thirty feet from our destination, I realized what had grabbed her attention. A blonde girl of about twelve or thirteen stood quietly next to her mother watching Raspberry's approach. The longing in her eyes made my heart ache. The dog plopped down in front of the girl and beat the sidewalk like a drum with her bony tail. The pretty blonde collapsed to her knees on the ground. She started to pet and hug and squeeze my dog. Raspberry soaked it up like a sponge, even the overzealous petting and too-hard squeezes.

The mother had tears in her eyes. "That's the nicest dog I've ever met. She didn't growl or slink back the way other dogs have."

"Why would they do that?" I asked.

"Hannah has some special needs, and I guess the way she walks kind of scares them."

"That must be why Raspberry was drawn to her then."

I saw questions in the woman's blue eyes. The same eyes I'd noticed in Hannah when we first walked up.

"This dog was raised in a home for special needs children," I said. "Other dogs might be frightened by an unusual gait or sudden movements, but to her it's normal, like being home."

"Oh, do you work at that school?"

"No. Raspberry doesn't get to live there anymore. Their board was terrified of the liability, so Raspberry was sent back to the breeder who resold her. She's a nice dog but she gets nervous in the show ring, and that's not what the judges like to see."

"Will you let us know if she's ever in a show around here?"

"We're in one next Saturday at the fairgrounds."

The next Saturday morning, I stood ringside trying to keep the butterflies in my stomach from flapping down the leash to Raspberry. If I really wanted to open a kennel, I needed to get a championship on her. We had to get fifteen points by beating other dogs in the ring. Most of the competition was well established and showing beautiful animals. Only the spectacular won. When a judge reached for Raspberry, she usually flinched—that little bobble, legacy of her puppy home—which took us out of the ribbons and sent hopes of my own kennel out into the future.

Our year together had helped. She no longer groveled in front of judges, but it wasn't enough. An Afghan hound is supposed to have a superior and aloof attitude; it should look down its very long nose at you. Raspberry looked up through her long white lashes with an expression of hope in her eyes and flinched when anyone reached for her.

All too soon the puppy class was out. It was our turn. "Come on, Razzle Dazzle." I did my best to make my voice light and happy. I reminded myself winning wasn't everything as we jogged into the ring. Raspberry's head hung near the floor. We weren't going to win this time either. I reached down and stroked her silky ear, wishing she understood my whispered "I love you."

Then it happened. Her head came up, her tail curled in a perfect ring over her back, and she was prancing around the circle in a motion that made her look like she was floating. The black-and-white hair flashed like changing storm clouds running before a strong wind. As the judge approached, she danced forward, wagged her tail, and gave a ladylike kiss to the reaching hand. No judge can resist a gentle little kiss. Smiling in spite of his attempts to hide it, the judge moved on to the other dogs in the ring. We did it. I waltzed out of the ring with a red second place ribbon, Raspberry's first ribbon ever.

> *Outside of a dog, a book is a man's best friend. Inside of a dog, it's too dark to read.*
>
> Groucho Marx

The ring steward called my number. The dog that beat us had won best of breed. Winning at a dog show is something of a pyramid competition, like the elimination rounds in a basketball tournament. All dogs compete in classes. The winners of the classes compete for best of breed. Each best of breed competes for best of group—hound, herding, working, terrier, toy, sporting, and nonsporting. The seven best in group dogs compete for best in show. A reserve winner is also selected in each competition, in case the best of breed dog can't compete or is disqualified from the group competition.

To make everything fair for the dogs that started in the same class with the best of breed winner, the second place winner is brought in to compete for reserve winner. Every second place handler stands ringside chewing their nails as they wait to see if they get to compete for second place in the breed showing. I wasn't any different. We had to go in and see which was second best.

Raspberry paraded back around the ring, and then I was handed the pink reserve winner's ribbon. I'm still not sure how we got out of there. As friends converged to congratulate us, Raspberry nearly jerked my arm off bolting for someone in the crowd. There stood Hannah. In a flash, Raspberry was up on her hind legs giving Hannah's face lots of dog kisses.

"Hi Raspberry, I knew you'd win. I just knew it. Mommy said since you're so nice, I can have a dog. I'm going to get one just like you."

Hannah's mother smiled at me. "I was wondering if you could tell me where to get a dog like Raspberry? Hannah hasn't stopped talking about her."

I hesitated. Was this a sign that Raspberry would be happier with Hannah than with me? I rubbed the silk ribbons, trying to decide what was best for this sweet dog. In that instant I think Raspberry read my mind. Dropping back to all fours, she romped over to me and leaned against my leg, looking up with love in her eyes.

It was my turn to be the mind reader. Raspberry was home. She would always love her special people, but I was her rock. She was happy in a world she trusted to stay the same with ice cream and show ribbons and me.

"Raspberry's breeder is here at the show. Let me introduce you."

I never saw Hannah or her mother again. I don't know if they bought a puppy or not. I'm just glad Raspberry made the opportunity possible.

I look through her show book sometimes. Most people who see it ooh and aah at all the blue and multicolor winners ribbons, but the red second place and pink reserve winner ribbons will always mean the most to me. That was the day Raspberry found the rock on which to build her home—love.

A Gift of Love

Ann H. Gabhart

I was nine years old when I got the dog hunger. I wanted a dog with every fiber of my being. I would have traded Christmas presents for the next five years, maybe even longer, if I could just have my own dog. I don't know whether a person is wired from day one to be a dog person or not, but if they are, I was. It wasn't that I didn't have plenty of animals I could call pets there on the farm. We had calves and lambs we bottle-fed and a barn crawling with cats. I loved my wooly lambs and the kittens, but I wanted a dog. A tail wagging, furry, wet-nose-in-your-face dog.

We'd had a dog, a big old hound we called Pup. When I was about six, he got hung in a fence and never came home. We hunted for him, but it was months before we knew what happened to him. He was a nice enough dog, but he was never my dog. You dog lovers out there know what I mean. And maybe I didn't have the dog hunger then.

I don't know why we didn't get another dog right away. Maybe my dad thought dogs were too much trouble, especially when they disappeared and made everybody sad. Anyway, I wasn't making any headway asking him for a dog, but I didn't quit asking. And praying. When I later wrote novels, one of my young characters says a dog prayer. That surely came straight from my heart and memory.

So after a few weeks of wishing and begging and praying, a dog showed up. Out of nowhere. A beautiful black cocker spaniel that was *my* dog at first sight. Only trouble was my dad couldn't see that. He said cockers didn't make good farm dogs and so we couldn't keep him. But I loved that little dog so desperately that my aunt took pity on me and gave the little dog a home. I named him Inky. It fit and he fit in my heart. Perfectly. My aunt and granddad lived about a mile from us. Every day all through that summer, I took the shortcut through the fields over to their house to sit on the porch beside my granddad, who was going on ninety, and let Inky lay his head in my lap while I stroked his soft curly hair. I was in love. Inky was in love. My dog hunger was satisfied, and I was happy. Very happy.

Alas, the course of true love never runs smooth. One day in late summer, after Inky had been in my life for a couple of months, my aunt and I came home from town to find at least a dozen dead hens scattered around the yard. Inky was hiding in the woodshed under a bench. He knew he'd done a bad thing. I knew he'd done a bad thing. He was a chicken killer. That's probably why somebody had dropped him out on the road in front of our farm to begin with.

My aunt loved me without reservation, but no farm woman could keep a chicken-killing dog. We needed eggs for breakfast.

I didn't care about the chickens or the eggs, but I understood that Inky's days were numbered in my life. They didn't shoot him. That was the best I could hope for. Instead my aunt tied him to the clothesline and found him a home with someone who didn't own chickens. And I lost my first love.

But the story doesn't end there. After Inky, my dad relented and let me have a dog. Ollie was part spitz and part collie, and I loved him as much as I'd loved Inky. Still, he wasn't a cocker spaniel. Forever after Inky, cocker spaniels were my dream dogs. But cocker spaniels didn't normally appear out of nowhere. They had to be bought. Something we never did when we wanted a dog. Something we couldn't afford to do after I married and had three kids. There wasn't money to *buy* a dog. When you wanted a dog, you found somebody trying to get rid of pups, and whatever kind they were, you took one and brought it home. But my husband knew how much I loved cocker spaniels. Because of how much he loved me, one year he sold his treasured high school class ring and bought me a cocker spaniel pup as a surprise for my birthday.

Three days before my birthday, my sister-in-law, Joy, was killed in a freak auto accident. A friend was driving her to the doctor since she was only days or perhaps hours from delivering her first baby boy. She and my husband's brother had three daughters already. The tailgate broke off a cattle trailer and crashed through the windshield of a pickup truck, instantly killing the driver whose wife, I found out later, was also about ready to have their baby. That truck crossed over into the path of the truck Joy's friend was driving. This was before seat belts were in common use, and Joy was thrown out of her seat and under the dashboard. The friend was not hurt, but Joy and her unborn baby boy died.

After that kind of tragedy, a birthday seems to be something to pass over, to not notice for this one year. How can you celebrate life when all you can think about is what death has stolen from your family? But my husband had already bought the puppy, and he brought him home to surprise me on my birthday in spite of the sadness that soaked clear through to my soul. Barely bigger than my hand, Jodie followed me everywhere I went and lay stretched across my foot whenever I was cooking or washing dishes. He was *my* dog at first sight.

The sadness and grief didn't go away because I had a puppy. I missed Joy and mourned the lost promise of the baby boy who never had a chance to draw breath. I was sad for the daughters who would grow up without their mother's loving presence. I grieved for Joy who would not see those girls become young women and marry and have babies of their own. But a puppy can lick away a lot of tears and make you smile in spite of your sorrows.

My husband didn't know such sorrows were waiting in the wings when he sacrificed something he treasured to give me a wiggling, yipping, wet-nose-in-my-face puppy. He just wanted to give me a gift of love. And he did.

Seventy Times Seven

Cindy Crosby

I'm a good hater and a slow forgiver. It took a dog to show me I was wrong.

He was a tricolor, collie-shepherd mix whose whole world was a cardboard refrigerator box with a short kennel run tucked behind a seedy motel. A rottweiler shared the same space. As the bitter months of winter bore down on Illinois, the two huddled together for warmth. But a cardboard box isn't much protection against the cold.

Someone alerted animal control, which came out and saw the two dogs braving the increasingly raw weather with so little shelter. The owner was warned that unless the dogs were given a better refuge, they'd be seized. The warnings were ignored.

When the January wind chills began their slow descent to thirty degrees below zero, animal control came for Max and his rottweiler friend. He and his dog pal were taken away from their rough "home"—perhaps the only one they'd ever known—and sent to the shelter, headed for euthanizing. At the shelter the two dogs were separated, but they barked so piteously for each other that they were finally put together. Collie Rescue, an animal help organization, was called. Could they take another collie? They came for Max, but they couldn't take his friend. Max barked and barked as the miles rolled between them. He would never see her again.

When Max was brought to us—his new foster home—he was a tattered version of a collie. Frostbite had nibbled away part of his beautiful tulip-shaped ears. His tail, injured in some unknown accident, was not the proud waving plume of a collie—it was just a stubby stump. A raging ear infection, which we began treating immediately, had already cost him much of his hearing.

It shouldn't have happened to a dog.

Max had a raw deal for nine years. At first we were leery. Would he be aggressive? Angry because of his ill treatment? How would he respond to our cat? He was our first foster rescue dog, and we were careful. Who knows what years of bad treatment will do to a dog?

Because of the ear infection and his lingering sadness over his missing pal, Max was lethargic. He'd lay between the family room and the kitchen, his furry body on the soft carpet, his long collie muzzle on the cool tile of the kitchen floor. Mysteriously, a pillow from our bed migrated to Max (I swore to my husband I had no idea how it got there), and he spent hours curled up on and around it.

As the days passed, our worries eased. Despite everything, Max had an open, sweet, trusting nature. Each person he met was a potential new friend. Whenever the neighborhood children saw me walking Max, they would drop their sleds and run over to give him a hug. His stump of a tail would quiver—his version of a joyful wag.

Max adored our elderly tabby cat, Socks, who grumpily refused to recognize his existence. Max would invite her to play. She'd take a swipe at his nose. Max didn't take it personally, and he never gave up. Eventually, she'd deign to let him lie down a few feet away from her without giving him the cold shoulder. He was winning her over.

Soon Max's ear infection cleared up. Good food and daily exercise gave him confidence and energy. A streak of collie mischief came into play. I'd hear a crash from the kitchen: Max was in the trash. Or I'd stroll into the living room to find Max guiltily clambering off the couch—where he wasn't allowed. He learned what a chew toy was for, and how to chase a ball and sit for a treat. He discovered the joys of peanut butter and chewing on an ice cube.

He was ready for a new home. Max's picture went up on the collie rescue website, and before two weeks had passed a potential adoptive family came to our house to meet him. I was nervous. Would they be good enough for Max? Would Max like them? The couple turned out to be a special education teacher and her husband, both close to retirement, both looking for an older dog to enjoy in their retirement years. Max greeted them by licking her on the face and laying his long collie muzzle in the man's lap.

I found myself strangely reluctant to give Max up. "You know he has hearing loss," I said. The woman laughed and pointed to her hearing aid. "We'll have something in common!"

Max needed a lot of veterinary care because of his ear infections, I told her, and I mentioned his age. "We're not sure he's only nine years old—he could be older," I cautioned.

The man told me how they had lost their fifteen-year-old collie just a year ago and missed him. "He couldn't walk anymore in his final few months, so we got him a doggie wheelchair so we could take him outside for walks," he said.

I made a last-ditch effort to be discouraging: "Max did have one accident in the house." The couple told me they had recently taken up all the carpet in their home, just to make it easier to clean up in case their new dog had an accident.

Then they asked me a question: "Does he like cats?" The couple had four, all pet rescue animals. At last—Max would have friends to play with again.

> *As long as a man has a dog, he has a friend. And the poorer he gets, the better friend he has.*
> Will Rogers

They were the ones. As much as it hurt to say good-bye to Max, it was the proverbial match made in heaven. But the house felt emptier when he was gone.

With his numerous losses, including his home and his best friend, Max was still ready to trust people. Even with his flaws—missing ear tips, cut-off tail, indiscriminate pedigree—Max still had a beauty all his own that came from a heart of gold. He was ready to fully love people again and again, even when they fell short and disappointed him or treated him unjustly. Max knew how to let go of the past without holding any grudges.

In Matthew 18:21–22, Peter asks Jesus, "Lord, how often should I forgive someone who sins against me? Seven times?"

"No, not seven times," Jesus replied, "but seventy times seven."

Seventy times seven. Sometimes it takes a dog to show you what's most important.

Share the Wealth

Sherri Gallagher

*I*t was Saturday, and I dialed Mom's number for our weekly phone call.

"Are you still looking for another Afghan hound?" she asked.

This was new. Mom had made her opinion abundantly clear that I needed another dog about as much as a homeless shelter needed another hungry mouth.

"Yes, why?"

"A lady on the bowling team said they were looking to get rid of theirs because they couldn't keep up the coat. If you're determined to get another dog, this one's free. And something is odd about the situation."

"Odd? How so?" Mom's intuition had been unusually accurate on more than one occasion.

"I don't know. I just have a feeling that dog needs out of there."

After I hung up the telephone, I went to find Jim, my husband of eight months. He called the telephone number, and I heard his side of the conversation. "I understand you have an Afghan hound you'd like to place in a new home. My wife and I would like to come meet him."

I sipped coffee and watched his jaw lock and his eyes begin to change color. Very bad sign. He was furious. "We're on our way up. It'll take about four hours to get there." Good thing the telephone was hard plastic. If it had been anything else, he would have squeezed it to a pulp. "Yes, I know it's raining," he said. "We'll be in the car. The dog is the one outside in it." He hung up the phone.

"Tell me," I asked, pouring coffee into a thermos and wrapping up the loaf of banana bread I'd just made.

"The dog has been chained outside to a doghouse with no floor all winter."

My hand shook, spilling the coffee. "We had a week where the temperature never got above zero. He's been out in that?"

"Yes."

It was a long four hours getting to the address we'd been given. Finally we saw it. A new house built in a muddy, raw gash on a hillside. Behind and above was a plywood doghouse. A large black creature stood at the end of his chain watching us.

The man came out and walked us up the hill. The picture we saw became more heartrending with every step. Mats the size of baseballs covered the dog, whose name we learned was Andi. He stood in a mire of mud and melting snow, and he wagged his tail. Fur had grown through and tangled in the piece of logging chain that had started as his collar and now slowly strangled him.

Jim reached out to release the dog, gently working the coat free. Our host chatted away, oblivious to the undercurrent of silent anger coming from my husband. "There's a school nearby, and if the kids don't like their lunch, they give it to the dog, so I don't bother to feed him too much. Afghans are supposed to be skinny."

Jim stood up straight, his hands involuntarily closing into fists. My husband had always believed in protecting those who can't defend themselves. I wondered if I was about to learn how to make bail and how much it would cost.

"Say," said the man, "if you're interested, I know where there's another Afghan hound that needs a home. They're having trouble with her coat too." Our host smiled at us.

My husband spoke to me through clenched teeth. "Dear, you get the information about that one. I'll wait in the car."

Jim walked Andi down the hill and loaded him in the backseat of our old sedan. Andi swallowed the remaining half a loaf of banana bread in one gulp. He spent the four-hour ride home stretched out in the backseat, occasionally releasing contented moans. It was the first time he'd been warm in months.

At the house, the minute he entered, he bolted for the large bowl of kibble left down for our Afghan puppy, Khan. We stopped Andi. If we let him gorge himself after eating so little for so long, he'd die a slow painful death.

"Go grab the bandages," Jim directed as he reached down to take the food away. "I'm about to get bit really bad, and I won't blame him at all." But Andi simply sat back on his haunches and whimpered as Jim swept the bowl out of reach. Jim scooped out a small amount of food and slowly fed the dog. "Let's see what we can do with this coat."

Somewhere near midnight we finished. We'd broken the clippers on stones stuck in his hair and had to complete the job with scissors. Without the long coat, it hadn't taken long to shampoo and dry Andi with the blow dryer. Every half hour we gave him a small scoop of food. Fortunately, a trip to the vet for shots along with a regimen of kibble mixed with baby formula and fed every two hours produced a miraculous recovery. The other Afghan hound Andi's previous owner mentioned had not been mistreated, and we quickly placed her into a loving home.

Andi decided Jim was his human. The dog followed him constantly and curled up in Jim's lap at every opportunity. Andi had been full grown and weighed fifty-four pounds when we collected him. He leveled out at eighty-six pounds and grew a glossy, pure black, wavy coat.

A little research showed him to be from a famous English kennel. He had been bought as a birthday present for a man who had no idea what to do with him and then given away to a secretary who seemed to adore the dog. It was her husband who had chained the dog outside while she had been busy with a new baby.

Our research showed there had originally been two lines of Afghan hounds. The smaller, lighter-colored desert hounds were used to hunt deer. The larger, darker-colored Afghans with wavy, coarser coats lived in the mountains and were sent out alone or in pairs to eliminate marauding wolves. Being from strong mountain stock had probably saved Andi's life. The only permanent damage was that the tip of his tail had been lost to frostbite.

The dog immediately recognized his improved conditions. That's not to say Andi didn't have his quirks. It took a few corrections to get him to stop lifting his leg on the Christmas tree. He apparently thought we brought it inside for use as a winter comfort station for canines. When Jim got involved in a big project and spent day and night hunched over his calculator, Andi dug it out of Jim's briefcase and chewed it into a pile of broken plastic and shattered circuit boards.

People don't think of Afghan hounds as protective, but that's a mistake. We lived in an apartment the first Halloween Andi spent with us. I had put the dogs in the bedroom while the doorbell rang and I passed out candy. As it got later, I turned down the lights and released the dogs. I heard a knock and opened the door to see a teenage boy decked out like a gangster, complete with a purple plastic machine gun. He got out "Trick or . . ." before I slammed the door and felt Andi sail over my shoulder, taking a chunk out of the doorjamb. A quick shuffle of dogs back to the bedroom, and I faced my adolescent wise guy. I donated all my remaining candy to his treasure bag.

No one had taught Andi to accept grooming, so we kept him neatly clipped. He accompanied us to the dog shows, watching from ringside while Khan pranced into the ribbons almost every show.

We were new to showing and didn't realize there was danger lurking in the air. That year a new disease had appeared and killed hundreds of show dogs. No one knew what caused it or spread it. Two dogs could be kenneled side by side. Ten days after the show, one would be dead and the other untouched. Dogs could come home from a show and not be sick, but a few weeks later almost every other dog in the kennel would die. It would later be identified as parvovirus, which travels through the air and is now prevented with a vaccine.

A week after we'd taken both Khan and Andi to a show, Khan started to run a fever. We rushed him to the vet and were told, "Call tomorrow and we'll tell you if he's survived."

We were lucky, Khan made it. After a week of IVs and round-the-clock care, Khan came home. We were warned his digestive system had been attacked, and we would have to feed him a soft, bland diet in small quantities.

By now Andi had long overcome his desire to gobble down every available morsel of food, and both dogs ate when they felt like it from a constantly full bowl of kibble. Since we were going to have to control Khan's intake, the bowl of kibble had to go away for a while.

We switched Andi to a bowl of moist food. We fed him alongside Khan and his spoonful of bland diet. Khan inhaled his dinner and lay down quietly next to his empty bowl while Andi slurped up what was usually a treat. Midgulp, Andi stopped and looked at Khan's empty bowl and his full one. He reached down and collected a large mouthful of food. Then he walked over to release it into Khan's empty dish.

I've never had a stomachache because I didn't have food. Sometimes it's easy to forget that the people next door may be starving when I have a full plate in front of me. Andi didn't forget. He shared with Khan and made me realize just how selfish I can be.

Andi has been gone for years now, but I make it a point to regularly drop off groceries at the local food pantry in memory of my compassionate dog.

Something a Lot like Love

Alison Hodgson

Almost as soon as I saw him, I knew something was wrong. My black Labrador puppy, Jack, was standing on the deck, licking the residue of vinegar and baking soda from the homemade rocket my son Christopher had set off the day before.

"Jack! No!" I shouted.

The dog looked up and blinked. It was then I noticed that he looked like his head had shrunk or that his body had bloated. I staggered back. That is what they call a visceral reaction.

My first thought was, "I *cannot* call the vet!" Then I had something like a near death experience, but it was Jack's short life that flashed before my eyes.

He was twelve weeks old when we brought him home on Good Friday, April 6. April 16 was his first visit to the vet, where I learned that—through a complete misunderstanding—I had been feeding him twice as much as necessary and he was on the brink of obesity. The owner of two Labs herself, the doctor recommended I replace his food bowl with something called a food cube, a plastic box that would require him to push and turn it over to dispense the food three or four kibbles at a time. She thought it would cost about $25.

I mentally put this at the bottom of my "to-buy" list. That month's budget was strained from the hundreds of dollars I had already spent on a dog crate, two pet gates, brushes, shampoos, a collar and tags, toys, a leash, examinations and vaccinations, pounds and pounds of food, the now deficient bowls, not to mention the dog himself.

April 27 we were back for more shots. Jack loved going to the vet. As soon as I opened the van door he was straining and pulling to get inside the office. From the very beginning I tried to teach him manners, so I made him wait while I entered first. This took time, energy, and strength. Jack is an English Lab, so he is stockier (even without overfeeding) and lower to the ground than the American line of the breed. It was like having a very small and demented bull on a leash. Since my kids loved to come along too, it was always a circus—monitoring them, controlling Jack, and answering any questions the staff had. I usually left the office with a headache and in a sweat. And this was a routine visit.

The morning of May 11 I called the vet because Jack had kept me up most of the night choking and gagging. Between his jags of coughing that should have brought up major organs, he was quite chipper. But the vet's office told me to bring him in immediately for examination. Jack didn't have any blockage, and after a thorough examination, the doctor suspected that he had literally inhaled a kibble. It worked its way out, but his trachea was irritated, causing him to cough.

For the examination, the sedation, and medication for his inflamed throat, the damage was $113.26 ($88.26 of which I recognized was stupid tax for not buying the food cube immediately after the vet recommended it). But I was happy to pay, having spent the night imagining what Jack might have swallowed (a stuffed animal, a large block, a long wool sock, an underwire bra, to name his favorite chews) and worrying that he needed extensive and expensive surgery . . . if he lived. I wasn't looking forward to dealing with my children's grief when Jack died someday, but five weeks after we got him was unthinkable.

"What are we going to do with you, Jackie Boy?" I said when we were home and resting on the lawn outside. He just stared at me and then quietly bit off a pansy from a nearby flowerpot. I didn't think it was toxic, but I swept it out of his mouth with my finger just to be safe.

On May 15, four days after his discharge, Jack was still coughing. I called the office. "Hi, this is Alison Hodgson—"

"How's Jack?" the receptionist asked. In eleven years with the same pediatrician, his receptionist still couldn't match me with my kids. I wasn't sure it was such a good thing that my vet's office knew my dog and me by name in less than a month.

May 18 we were back in for his last round of shots, and I scheduled Jack to be neutered on June 22. After that he and my checkbook would be free for a year.

May 29 I called to ask about a cut on his mouth that had stopped bleeding, but I wondered if I needed to or if it was even safe to apply Neosporin. They told me it was safe but that he would only lick it off. Since the bleeding had stopped he was probably okay, but I was to keep an eye on his eating and drinking.

June 9, a Saturday, Jack began limping for no apparent reason. There was no way I was going to call the office on the weekend. I decided to keep an eye on him and hoped he would get better.

The following Monday, June 11, he was still limping, so I reluctantly called. Since there was no known trauma, they told me to continue monitoring him and to try to limit his activity. I needed to call if it got any worse or if it hadn't improved any by the end of the week.

The next morning when I walked outside and was startled by the sight of my ludicrously swollen dog licking the deck, I didn't think I could take it anymore. Another call to the vet—however kind and understanding everyone there had always been—was unbearable. I took another look at Jack. He blinked at me placidly. He was fine, I decided.

Despite this staunch declaration and my firm resistance to calling the vet, I kept an uneasy eye on him throughout the day. At one point I even did a kind of examination, pressing his sides, feeling for his ribs.

My sister Torey called, and I told her the latest installment in the saga of Jack. "I'm sure he's fine," I told her. "I couldn't call the vet *again*. They probably think I have Munchausen's syndrome by proxy . . . with a dog."

"What?"

"You know, that syndrome where parents pretend their kids are sick to get attention—Munchausen's by proxy—except they're going to think I have it with Jack. I wonder if there is such a thing with pets."

The kids and I were outside most of the day, and Jack was always right with us. I did notice that he seemed to be panting a bit more than normal, and he was certainly drinking a lot of water, but I attributed that to the warmth of the day. That is what they call denial.

When my husband, Paul, came home, it was the normal mayhem of kids running to greet him and the dog barking on the periphery. "Paul, take a look at Jackie Boy, would you?" I asked.

We both turned to look at the dog who was standing in the kitchen doorway. I gasped. His body looked twice its normal size and his large blockish head appeared tiny in comparison. His expression was strained.

"That ain't right," Paul said.

"Do you think I should call the vet?"

"Um, yeah."

I ran to get the phone. A recording answered saying that the office was closed, but I waited to leave a message. "This is Alison Hodgson—"

The receptionist picked up the phone. "How's Jack?" she asked.

I told her.

She asked me a few questions and then put me on hold to check in with one of the doctors. A minute later she was back.

"The doctor is very concerned and recommends you take him to the emergency clinic." She gave me the number. "I hope he's okay," she said with genuine concern. My sister rushed over to stay with the kids, and Paul and I left with Jack.

At the clinic they admitted Jack right away. One of the doctors met with us privately. She recommended starting with X-rays. A little while later she came back, pictures in hand, and attached one to the light box. Jack's spine was immediately recognizable flowing across the top of the X-ray. I could see it was a profile shot of his hindquarters, but that was about it. The doctor pointed to a large, oblong, cottony mass. Had Jack scarfed down a bag of cotton balls? I didn't think we owned that many.

"What is that?" I asked.

"It appears to be kibble."

It looked like there were hundreds and hundreds.

I looked at Paul. "I don't know when he could have eaten all that." Paul shook his head. Neither of us knew. We'd been asked here and by our doctor if Jack could have gotten into his food, but I didn't think he had. The food was stored in the laundry room, which was down a hall off the kitchen, and the door was always shut. Since Jack was always underfoot—my feet in particular—I couldn't think of a time that he had been in the laundry room. But clearly he had.

The doctor laid out her plan. The first step was to induce vomiting. Hopefully that would be successful. If not, the next step would be a gastric lavage in which Jack, under sedation, would have a tube slid down his esophagus into his stomach and they would pump the food out.

"He's going to have his stomach pumped?" I asked. It was such a melodramatic phrase. I never expected it to be associated with my puppy.

"Hopefully not, but yes, that's what gastric lavage is," the doctor replied.

Hopefully not indeed! Every step of Jack's care we were given an estimate of the cost of each proposed treatment. We knew that just getting him in the door to be examined and X-rayed, we were already up around $250. The less they did now, the cheaper it was.

We went out to the grim waiting room where the only reading material was a couple of ancient *Pet Fancy* magazines and a large photo album featuring the clinic's staff. After we had read the magazines cover to cover and were practically part of the Animal Emergency Hospital family, we were called back to the private room.

The doctor got right to it: they were not able to induce vomiting. Our options were to go ahead with the gastric lavage or take Jack home and hope the food would pass normally. The risk in taking him home was that the food would harden and rupture the stomach, necessitating emergency surgery.

I leaned forward. "How much is the gastric lavage?" I asked.

The doctor repeated the financial range of the procedure.

"And what are we up to now with the induction?"

The doctor gave me a ballpark number on our tab and then left us alone to talk.

I added the two and shook my head. "I have never been in an emergency where I have asked the price of medical care. What do you think?" I asked Paul.

"I think we should do it," he replied. "We're already in this far, and I want it to be resolved tonight. When we take Jack home, I want to know that he's okay."

I agreed and we told the doctor.

Although I had been the one to first suggest getting a puppy, it was only because I thought it would be good for the children. It never occurred to me that a dog could be good for me too. Paul had resisted initially and only agreed after we had thought and prayed about it for a very long time. Paul became the one to immediately fall in love with Jack. For me, Jack was worry and constant work. He was also adorable and sweet, but the former far outweighed the latter.

Since he had been admitted, we could hear him barking almost nonstop in the back of the clinic, and I felt a new and strange pull of tenderness for that silly and troublesome dog. When his barking quieted, we knew the sedation had taken effect and that the gastric lavage was underway.

Time passed so slowly in that dismal waiting room. Finally, almost five hours after he had been admitted, Jack was ready to go home. He staggered out, but his tail was wagging. We winced when he was close enough to smell. Rancid, fetid, malodorous, putrid, noxious, rank, foul—I need all these words to describe the height, the width, and the breadth of that odor. And vile, definitely vile.

In the car I sat with him in the backseat. He lounged across my lap and stuck his nose out the window I had rolled down as far as it would go, and he sniffed the air. Paul looked back at us and smiled. "Jackie Boooooooy!" he crooned. Jack pulled his head back in and his tail thumped against the seat.

I wish I could say that this was the last of Jack's mishaps and emergencies. The most dramatic and expensive, but alas, not the last.

Who could know that he would have a strange reaction to the anesthesia when he was neutered (June 22), making him hyper and frantic instead of sleepy as expected, and that he would bash his large cone into everything, particularly my shins, for the better part of a week; that he would leap onto the counter and eat an unknown amount of chocolate chips (June 26); that he would fall off our deck (July 16) and develop another limp requiring X-rays and medication; that he would make another dash for the laundry room (August 9) and scarf down a day's worth of food before I dragged him away; that his limp would return again (August 22) and again (December 27); that he would swallow a rubber yo-yo (April 9 the following spring) necessitating another induction of vomiting.

And who could know that Paul and I would begin to get up together early every morning to walk Jack for his good and find that in so many ways it was for our good too; that all of us would laugh and play as a family even more; and that somewhere in the midst of those visits and calls, month after month in the day-to-day keeping of that dog, I would begin to deeply care for him, rather than simply take care of him.

My pastor says to know a person's priorities, you only have to look in her checkbook register. The Bible says where your heart is your treasure will be. Well, Jackie Boy was in my checkbook, depleting my treasure, long before he was in my heart. And driving home from the emergency clinic that warm spring night, as he slouched against me, I could feel his heart beating and his tail wagging and the beginning of something a lot like love.

The Rescued Dog Who Rescued Me Back

Shanna Verbecken

It's a few days after Christmas as I tell this story. Six weeks ago, the week before Thanksgiving, I lost almost everything. But I'm a blessed woman today, thanks to my dog, Ladybug.

I met Ladybug several years ago at a shelter near my home. I was looking for a dog, although that day I was only window-shopping because I did not have money to adopt. But there was this little thirteen-week-old puppy, a mix of black Labrador retriever, Irish setter, and greyhound. Think of a black dog built like a small greyhound with a sweet disposition. That's Ladybug.

I fell in love with her, but what bad timing. The shelter people told me this puppy was going to be put down the next day unless someone adopted her. I wanted to adopt her, but it would cost me $50 and I did not have it. Right then that was a lot of money to me.

At the time, I was waiting tables on the midnight shift in a truck stop restaurant. The economy was already bad and soon to get worse, so business wasn't great, which means nobody was rolling in tip money. I met the dog on a Tuesday, which is not the best time of the week for tips. But when I went to work that night, I told myself if I pulled in the $50 in tips, I'd get the dog in the morning.

We were just as slow that shift as I figured we'd be, and I only wrote six tickets all night. How I got $50 in tips on six tickets I have no idea, but I did. That was my first miracle.

So when I left work in the morning, I hurried to the shelter. The dog saw me and ran right to the gate, dancing in circles. What a joy! I named her Ladybug in memory of my fiancé Bob's childhood dog.

Right from the start Ladybug went everywhere with me. If I rattled my keys, she would dance with delight, ready to go. She was a snuggler who slept with me at night. She was always alert and aware of her surroundings, and I felt very safe with her around.

I had met my fiancé, Bob, the same year I got Ladybug, so that was a good year all around for me. He was a long-distance truck driver, a customer I met while working at the truck stop restaurant. I noticed he was coming in more frequently, and eventually we started dating. Then the day came when he proposed to me right there in the restaurant in front of about thirty people.

We started planning our wedding. I have grown children and grandchildren, so this was going to be a very happy occasion for my family and me. The week before Thanksgiving, Bob and my family moved all my things into a new mobile home. Then Bob took off that day for a cross-country haul.

That night I would be spending my first night in my new home. My daughter and my little baby grandson were going to join me for my first night, but at the last minute she called to say that the baby had a fever. Reluctantly, they stayed home. So for my first night in my new home, it would just be Ladybug and me and my two long-haired cats, Gizzy and Mickey, who both adored Ladybug.

I took a shower, crawled into bed, and watched the eleven o'clock news. The sounds and smells of a new home were different, of course, but I didn't hear or smell anything odd. Ladybug and the cats parked on the bed with me. I take pain medication at night for a back injury, and that makes me sleep very hard, especially at first. So soon enough I was sound asleep.

I had been sleeping a couple of hours when I became aware of something brushing my face. When you sleep with cats, this isn't unusual, and I didn't rouse for it. Then I felt Ladybug hit my chin. This was unusual, but I was pretty numb from medication and I didn't rouse for Ladybug hitting my chin either.

The next thing I knew, my gentle Ladybug had my collar in her teeth, pulling on it and growling. That woke me up. I opened my eyes, disoriented. I sat up, and that's when I saw that the end of my bed was on fire. Flames were literally shooting up from the blankets.

I scrambled out of bed, but I wasn't used to my surroundings so I stumbled around with Ladybug for a few seconds. I felt my way away from the bed, around the dresser, and into the hallway. It was so dark in the hallway I couldn't see my hand in front of my face. I knew I had to get outside but I was still disoriented.

Then I remembered, as is often the case in long mobile homes, there was a back hallway door to the outside. Ladybug had stayed at my side, but I couldn't find my cats. Now instead of getting out while the flames got worse, I was trying to figure out how to rescue my pets.

Ladybug and I finally got outside. I momentarily hoped that if I left the door open, the cats would find their way out. But in my agitation, I turned and went back in to find them. Fortunately my neighbor Donna ran onto the porch and inside after me, yelling for me to get out. She had pulled her coat up over her face to go into the living room and get me. She literally pulled me through the door to the outside.

I jumped away from her. I was running on automatic and a little crazy right then, and a couple of teenage girls stopped me from running back in the place again. Donna convinced me to move away from the burning building, and one of my neighbors told me, "You're going to be okay." Everyone assured me that Ladybug and one of my cats, Mickey, were out and okay—the teenage girls had taken both the dog and the cat to their house.

Outside I became aware that it was freezing cold. The fire trucks had taken a little longer to arrive because of the icy roads, but now they were there and began doing their work. I looked at my home. It was fully engulfed in flames. *It's gone,* I thought. *Everything Bob and I have been working for is gone. Are we ever going to get anywhere?* I stood and watched and listened. The firefighters threw a burning mattress out. It was the mattress I had been sleeping on. That's when I passed out.

When I came to, I was on the sidewalk with an oxygen mask over my face. I was aware of being very cold, and then I realized again what was happening. Now I thought about all my family pictures inside the house—my children's pictures, my grandchildren's. My dad had died a few years earlier, and I knew where his pictures were, all inside a zipped plastic bag. I was very close to my dad, and those pictures meant a lot to me. I made crazy motions to get up. Then the chief of police got firm with me and put me in his patrol car.

A neighbor man I didn't know walked up with Ladybug on a leash. The officer opened the car, and the man said to me, "Your dog is trying to find you—she's been whining and howling and trying to tear my door down." Ladybug hopped in the car with me, her tail thumping. "I have your cat at my house too," the man said. I was very grateful.

Ladybug settled right down and leaned against me while we watched the firemen work on what had been our new home. I checked her over. Her eyelashes and eyebrows were singed, and so was one side of her whiskers. Otherwise she was fine, and we were together, safe.

While I sat in the patrol car, someone called Bob. He was several hours away, driving westbound on the Indiana Toll Road. I'm sure he annoyed a lot of people when he U-turned that big rig to drive eastbound and get back to me.

While my cat Mickey was safe with the neighbors, I was afraid my other cat Gizzy hadn't made it. But that night the chief of police and my future brother-in-law found Gizzy inside the burned mobile home—miraculously alive and well! She had hidden behind a piece of floorboard we had propped up against the living room wall, and she'd pressed her face into a towel on the floor. It saved her life.

The next day, officials went over the damage. Everything synthetic had melted, even the shower stall. Bob was allowed to help them look for my family pictures—and they found them. My kids' pictures were protected by the album they were in, which oddly had not burned. The photos are glued in there permanently, but they're there. They found my dad's photos intact. Because of the move, all these pictures had been wrapped in an afghan. That melted, but the pictures were okay. I also had a jewelry box that burned, but a heart-shaped pendant that says *Mother* sat untouched in that jewelry box, encased in solid ice.

The officials discovered that the wires beneath the mobile home had been tampered with and crossed the entire length of the structure. They still don't know who did this, and the investigation is still open. The fire chief told me, "If it wasn't for the dog, you would have been overcome by toxic smoke in a matter of minutes." Praise God for Ladybug.

I can't say I'm not affected by this, because I am. I need a light on when I sleep. Where I live now, neighbors heat with wood, and the smell of that smoke bothers me. Whenever freezing rain hits the window, it sounds to me like the boards popping in the fire. But Ladybug sticks close by. She's my guardian in fur.

My kids ask me what I want for Christmas. I have the best gift, because I have life. I lost everything material in that fire except for pictures, a few dishes, and what I had on my back. But I have my animals, I have my family, and I have Bob, who recently gave me a diamond.

My folks always taught me to be a fighter. As I watched my life go up in flames, I had a moment when I thought, *I've been fighting so much, and I just get knocked down over and over.* But then I could hear my dad saying, *You're strong. You're going to make it. Now smile and keep your chin up.*

So that's what I do, gratefully, with Ladybug at my side.

Skippy

Gwen Ellis

I suppose in every lifetime there is one special animal that
makes a lasting impression. In my life that animal was
Skippy. We didn't adopt him. He adopted us.

My mom was working as an accountant at the Ford Motor
Company in Deer Lodge, Montana. One day, one of the
company's salesmen came in from the car lot complaining
about a dog that kept getting into the cars and sleeping on
the seats. Mom went to see what they were talking about.
She found a black-and-white fox terrier mix right where the
salesman said it would be—asleep in a car. He appeared to
be healthy, friendly, and intelligent.

Mom went back inside and called my dad to see if she
could bring the dog home. I think Daddy was reluctant, but
he finally said yes. When Mom arrived home that evening,
the dog was with her. We named him Skippy.

Skippy settled right in as if he'd always been with us, and
Daddy's reluctance about having a pet melted away immediately.

Within a few days, the two became fast friends, and they stayed friends for many, many years until Skippy's death.

Skippy was probably the most intelligent animal I had ever known. And he had soul too. If you praised him, he got it right away. If you shamed him, he got that right away as well. He knew lots of tricks, which he learned after being shown how to do them only a few times. When he arrived at our house, he was skinny, smelled bad, and was extremely tired. He was assigned a place under the kitchen counter where he could sleep. It was right in the middle of the family's activities, yet he was out of the way. He liked his place immediately and went willingly to his rug at the end of each day.

After we'd had Skippy for a time, my brother acquired some rabbits to raise. One day, one of the expectant mother rabbits got out of the hutch and delivered her babies in some soft grass near the garage. We didn't know she had gotten out of the hutch, but Skippy did. Fox terriers didn't get their name by lying around on silken pillows in a king's palace. They are hunting dogs and will go into a barking frenzy when chasing prey.

Skippy came to the house to get Daddy. The dog fussed and whined and stewed. He followed at Daddy's heels until Daddy finally turned to him and said, "What is it? Do you want me to follow you?" Skippy jumped around, ran a few feet in the direction of the garage, and came back. "All right, I'm coming," Daddy told the worried dog, who was already running toward the garage.

Skippy ran straight to a pile of naked baby rabbits with their eyes sealed tight and bulging in their tiny skulls. Skippy could have killed all of them at the same time with one bite. Instead, he stood whining and looking at Daddy.

"Well, I'll be . . ." Daddy said. He took off his cap and carefully lifted the babies into it. He carried them back to the hutch. It didn't take long to locate the mother rabbit, catch her, and return her to the safety of her cage. Skippy had denied his natural hunting instincts to rescue our baby rabbits.

That experience taught us a lot about our little dog. Later on, we understood how truly amazing it was that he had sought help for the baby bunnies. We were coming home from an outing when a huge jackrabbit dashed in front of our pickup. Jackrabbits are about a foot tall and they have ears that are about another foot tall. They look gigantic. Daddy stopped the car as the rabbit ran to the side of the road.

Skippy saw the rabbit too. He leaped out the window and chased after that jackrabbit. We got out of the truck and called and called. He either didn't hear us or didn't want to hear us. The last thing we saw was a jackrabbit disappearing over the hill followed closely by a frantic black-and-white fox terrier.

We kids were very upset. We figured we had seen the last of our dog. We continued calling, but there was no answer. We had just about given up when a head poked up over the horizon. It was Skippy. This time when we called him, he took one last look back to where the rabbit disappeared and then came trotting down the hill to us. He was hot and panting. He crawled into the car, lay down on the floor by an air vent, and stayed very still the rest of the way home. We knew then how strong his natural instinct was to give chase, and that made the miracle of his protecting the baby rabbits even more amazing.

Neighbors who lived two doors down the street got a collie pup. The collie's name was . . . you guessed it . . . Lassie. We watched her grow from a roly-poly puppy to a beautiful, golden, long-haired adult. She and Skippy became fast friends. Every day she would come to the window of our dining room, stick her nose against the glass, and grin. We would let Skippy out, and they would roughhouse and tumble all over the yard with the glee of young kids let out of school.

That went on for a couple of years. Then one day, Skippy once again started bugging Daddy to get his attention. He whined and ran a few feet and came back.

By this time, Daddy was well trained. He turned to Skippy and said, "What's wrong? Do you want me to follow you?" Skippy let him know that he did. Daddy followed Skippy to the neighbor's yard. There lay Lassie. She had been hit by a car and was dying. Skippy had done the only thing he knew how to help his friend. He had run home to get someone he could trust and had brought him to her. Skippy grieved Lassie's death. He never did have another friend like her.

> *You will always win more friends by wagging your tail than your tongue.*
> Anonymous

Skippy liked to help my dad. When Daddy planted potatoes in the early spring, he dug holes in the ground and dropped in the pieces of potato that would grow into plants. One day, when he was halfway down a row, he looked behind him. There was Skippy, covering up every piece of potato and filling every hole.

Once Daddy was repairing the roof of our house. He was way out on the front eaves, twenty-five feet from the ground. He was concentrating on his work when something warm and wet touched his neck. It's a wonder he didn't fall off the roof. Slowly, he turned his head to see what had touched him. There stood Skippy wagging his tail. He had climbed the ladder, crawled over the ridge of the house, and now stood next to Daddy. He'd come to help. He couldn't climb down the ladder. Daddy had to get up carefully, pick up the dog, climb back down the slope of the roof, and then climb down the ladder. In the future, he pulled the ladder up on the roof to keep Skippy from climbing it.

Perhaps one of the most poignant moments of this little dog's amazing activities came when we were on vacation. Skippy never stayed in a kennel. He went everywhere with us. We were in Minnesota when my brother Glen became ill. He was so sick that we feared for his life. No one knew what was wrong with him. The doctors in that town suggested Mom and Dad take Glen to the Mayo Clinic in Rochester—a town that was nearby. They took him there and he was hospitalized.

My brother Ray and I stayed with my aunt. We silently prowled around her house, too afraid to talk about what was happening to our brother. Skippy was with us at my aunt's house while we waited to hear if Glen was going to live. I moped, Ray moped, and Skippy moped with us.

When Mom and Dad came home from the hospital that first night, they needed to pray about this desperate situation. They looked for a place to pray and others who would pray with them. They found a small congregation who gladly joined them in prayer for my brother. There was no fanfare or call from the hospital with good news that my brother's condition was improved, but when my parents came back from prayer, Mom said, "I know he will be all right."

And he was. The next morning when Mom and Dad returned to the hospital, miraculously Glen was sitting up and working jigsaw puzzles. After a few more days in the hospital for recovery and observation, he was released. His diagnosis was mumps, meningitis, and encephalitis—all three. It would take him a long time to recover.

The doctors thought Mom and Daddy would have to get an ambulance to take Glen home to Montana—a distance of a thousand miles. It just so happened that we had a homemade camper on the back of the pickup we were traveling in. The doctors thought that as long as Glen could lie down (there was a good-sized bed in the truck), it would be all right for him to go home that way.

We loaded up the truck and headed for the hospital. Mom and Dad went in and signed Glen's release papers, and then they brought him out in a wheelchair. When Daddy opened the door to the back of the camper, Skippy saw Glen. While Ray and I held onto his collar with all our might, Skippy strained to reach Glen. Skippy had known all along that something was wrong. He knew someone was missing. He knew that being together with his family—his whole family—was just about the best thing that could happen to a small black-and-white fox terrier.

Skippy died long after all of us kids had grown up and left home. Whenever we return to Montana, we can almost see him out chasing rabbits, helping Daddy plant potatoes, or wagging his tail furiously in absolute delight that we have come home. He will always be alive in our hearts.

Vicki

Kelly Pickett Bishop

It had already been a long night, and my husband, Charlie, wasn't looking forward to the rest of it. His job of repossessing cars was usually something he enjoyed, but there were always repos he wished he didn't have to do. He'd just had one of those. Knowing he was taking a necessity from someone was difficult, but those were the rules.

Charlie backed the truck up carefully. As he angled to make sure he was aligned with the back of the repossessed car to make loading easier, he saw a flash of white under the car in his side mirror. He finished pulling the truck in but decided he should check out what he had seen before going any further.

He leaned down and shined his flashlight under the car. There was an animal—too big to be a cat but not quite big enough to be a dog. He saw the eyes reflecting the light back at him, and in them he saw fear and uncertainty. He got down on his stomach to look closer and then realized it *was* a dog. And not a healthy one, judging by what he could see.

Charlie was unsure how to proceed. The dog looked like a pit bull, and this could wind up ending badly. He inched his hand forward, palm down, and started murmuring gently to the animal. Unsure, it started to retreat with something in its mouth. Charlie quietly asked his partner to grab his midnight snack of beef jerky out of the cab of the truck. Once Charlie had it opened in his hand, the dog caught the scent. It was obvious that the dog was struggling with the decision of whether to flee or to accept the offer. It crawled tentatively toward Charlie, the smell proving irresistible.

Charlie backed up slowly, trying to entice the dog out from under the vehicle. Eventually they met at the curb, the dog dropping the orange peel it had been eating and daintily taking the beef jerky from Charlie's hand. He could see that the dog wasn't well. She was a female and so skinny you could easily count her ribs just by sight. She was definitely a pit bull, and she was so emaciated she could have been an advertisement for animal abuse and neglect.

As Charlie gently petted her head, she made eye contact, and the sadness and fear were immediately visible. She nudged his hand again with her head, asking for more affection. She seemed to recognize his good intentions, and she decided to trust him. Charlie knew that if he dropped her off at a police station or animal control, she would be put down because of her breed. It was decision time.

The apartment Charlie and I rented with our two children didn't allow pets; the landlord had been very clear on that issue. But maybe, Charlie figured, if he just brought the dog home and cleaned her up, he could find a home for her or a rescue organization that would keep her alive.

He turned his back to the dog and walked toward the truck. He was surprised to find her right behind him every step of the way. When he opened the door of his truck, she looked at him as if asking for permission. He nodded his head and said, "C'mon, girl, in the truck," and she hopped in without question. Charlie wondered whether I would hug him or kill him, but he knew he had no choice. He could not leave the dog here, ill and struggling.

She curled up on the seat between Charlie and his partner, content to snooze while they finished their shift. After returning to the shop with them, she followed him without question to his own car and once again looked to Charlie for the okay to get in. She calmly sat down and waited to find out what was next.

When Charlie arrived home I was just getting up for the day, and he told me to come outside, that he had brought something home. Knowing my husband, I fully expected it to be a computer or some new toy for him to tinker with. Instead I found myself staring into eyes that held so much pain and fear it brought tears to my own. Charlie looked at me and said, "I couldn't leave her there . . . she was so scared, and she looks so sick. I had to do *something*."

I smiled at my husband and asked if she was friendly, important because of our two young children. Charlie said he'd seen nothing to indicate she wasn't. So we opened the truck door. The dog jumped down gracefully and sat, apparently waiting for further instruction, unsure of what was expected of her. I said gently, "Okay, let's go in the house," and we started up the steps. The dog followed. She seemed to know she would be okay here.

We found a vet who could see her that morning. She weighed in at only seventeen pounds. With her being so malnourished, the best estimate the vet could give on her age was somewhere around one year old. Other than being underweight, she appeared to be healthy. We took her home and named her Vicki.

We knew we couldn't keep her, but neither of us was ready to let go of her. There was just something about her personality that made you love her on sight. She was skittish, sudden noises made her tremble, new people made her nervous. She appeared to perk up some with our kids. We introduced her to David, our seven-year-old, and she curled up at his feet, content to be near a human.

Next was the most important meeting. Chris, our three-year-old disabled son, spent the majority of his time rolling around on the floor. Vicki gently sniffed his body and his face as if she knew she needed to be extremely careful. She found the edge of his blanket and lay there watching him. And then she refused to move. She quickly learned that an alarm coming from one of his monitors meant that a human was needed, and she took on the job of alerting us, just in case we missed it. She somehow taught herself to recognize when Chris was having a seizure, and she made sure that she got the attention of a human to handle the situation.

No leash was needed to walk her. Out the door, she would make her energy run around the yard, do what she needed to do, and return to the door immediately, despite there being no fence to keep her there. A month or two passed, and though we knew in theory that we couldn't keep her, we didn't make much effort to find her a home.

At her next visit to the vet, Vicki weighed in at a healthy forty-seven pounds. Had Charlie not found her that night, she probably would not have survived. She, along with the rest of us, had decided that she was home. We were her humans, and she was part of the family. When the landlord put his foot down and said she had to go, one of Chris's nurses said she would take Vicki. Though it broke our hearts, we agreed, with one stipulation—if there ever came a time when they couldn't keep her, for whatever reason, they would call us and we would take her back, no questions asked.

After three months, that phone call came. According to the nurse, Vicki was destructive, tearing up blankets and barking incessantly. They brought her back that afternoon, and that was when we found out why she was being such a "problem." They had been keeping her in a cage in the basement for hours and hours each day. This dog, who had been abused and neglected from an early age, was given a taste of a real life with a real family, only to be thrown back into neglect.

The day she came back, we started looking for a new place to live, one that would be willing to accept our *entire* family, including Vicki. She is the protector of her family, of her humans. She will place herself in front of Chris's wheelchair, and the decision of who can access him is hers. She recognizes how frail he is and that she needs her protection the most. Now Vicki is loved, treated like the princess she is, and given full run of acres of land. She is able to do what she perceives is her job—taking care of her pack.

You Just Never Know

Catherine Ulrich Brakefield

*M*ommy, can I have her?" Kimmy's face beamed up at me as she hugged an ebony puppy with a white spot marking its chest and big, bearlike paws patting her hand playfully.

Flashbacks of my youth and the puppies I enjoyed cantered through my thoughts. I suddenly realized I was the same age as my daughter, just five years old, when I received my first puppy. That puppy had playfully introduced me to a life of caring.

"We'll name her Dixie," I said. Surely naming this puppy in tribute to my husband's beloved South would work a miracle on him too. I needed one. We already had three cats, a bunny, and four horses.

The owner said the three puppies left were ten weeks old and free. *And very close to losing their puppy appeal*, I thought. The puppy's mother was a Labrador and springer spaniel mix. The father was unknown. I sighed, wishing I hadn't told my daughter we'd take her and thinking, *My daughter's puppy is a mutt.*

Kimmy attempted to place Dixie, who had to be a hefty fifteen pounds, on her lap. Dixie made do as best she could, her tail creating miniclouds of dust slapping the ground, reciprocating my daughter's act of friendship by licking the smudges of peanut butter and jelly from her cheek.

"Mommy, she likes me," Kimmy said, giving Dixie a big hug.

Dixie soon wagged her way into my husband's heart and mine, and the months happily sped along. Then I realized that Dixie was gaining an awful lot of weight. No one noticed when Dixie grew to maturity, but everyone noticed when Dixie grew rounder. *How does one explain the facts of life to a dog?* I frowned and asked, "Dixie, you should have known better. Now, just who is he?"

Dixie barked, placed two paws in front, and barked again. She appeared proud of herself, and I couldn't help smiling. Dixie yelped again, grabbing her ball and bringing it to me for a game of fetch.

I rubbed her ears. "So you had fun romping with your boyfriend, but just where is he now?"

August came in with escalating temperatures. When her time of delivery drew near, Dixie chose the north side of the house, panting in the shade.

"Mommy, Dixie won't play. Is she sick?"

"No, Kimmy, she's going to have puppies. Be very careful. Don't lean on her tummy."

"Oh?" Kimmy said, suddenly all eyes as she put a curious hand on Dixie's enlarged abdomen. "How many are in there?"

"Oh, probably a half dozen. And if their father is that short-haired pointer up the street, it could be as many as ten, maybe even fifteen."

"Oh!" she gasped, clearly awed.

Together we chose a nice corner in our basement. I lined the floor with papers and then laid layers of towels down. Kimmy became so excited that she could hardly take time to eat. Even the daily routines of play and church became complicated. Then one evening Dixie did not come romping back to our calls.

"Dixie! Here, Dixie! Did you check the stables, Edward?"

My husband's search yielded nothing.

That night the sound of thunder rumbled outside, and lightning lit the sky. A torrential downpour covered the windowpanes, matching the tears streaming down my cheeks. As everyone slept, I sat curled in my chair, waiting out the night with my Bible on my knees as I thought about the evening's events. What had happened to Dixie? I was worried. But I knew that God cares what happens to even the least of his creation.

"Dixie!"

I rushed to the kitchen the next morning as Kimmy opened the door to a much thinner dog. Dixie hurried toward her bowls of water and food. She lapped up the water in huge gulps.

"Close the door, Kimmy." I poured more lukewarm water into Dixie's empty bowl. "Now listen to Mommy: we're going to have to leash Dixie before we let her out; that way we won't lose her when she goes to her puppies. So honey, don't open the door until I tell you to, okay?"

"Okay, Mommy."

I hurried toward the laundry room and reached for the box full of dog and cat collars and leashes. Then I paused before leaving the room, grabbing one of Kimmy's worn blankets out of the laundry pile. *This will do for the puppies*, I thought. Then I heard the back door open. "Kimmy!"

I made it just in time to see Dixie bolt out the door with something yellow in her mouth.

"Kimmy, what did Mommy say—why did you let Dixie out?"

"But Mommy," Kimmy said tearfully, "Dixie was whining. She—had to go outside to her bathroom . . ."

Realizing I, too, was very close to tears, I hugged Kimmy. "Okay now, don't cry. We'll find her."

"But Mommy, Dixie's got my Winnie-the-Pooh bear in her mouth—she wouldn't let me have it," she whimpered. "I want my Winnie-the-Pooh."

"Dixie won't hurt it. Now let's get our raincoats and boots on."

With leash, dog biscuits, and Kimmy's old blanket, I was ready to spend the day in the woods finding our delinquent dog's offspring. As we rounded the corner of the house, Dixie came bounding up to us, Kimmy's Winnie-the-Pooh clasped between her jaws.

"Good Dixie! Good girl! Come here, let's just put this on . . ." But Dixie would not let me get close enough to her to put her leash on, nor would she drop Winnie-the-Pooh. With every step we took, she kept the same distance between us.

Deep into the belly of the woods we went, descending into the marshlands. The crack of twigs echoed in the hushed stillness, and the roots of decayed trees made a challenging obstacle course for Kimmy. Usually this area was swampy, but the dry summer had left some areas murky and others parched even after last night's rain. I wrapped the blanket around my neck and reached down. "Here, let Mommy carry you."

"No, I want to walk."

I looked at my stubborn offspring then back to her dog. Exhausted, I patiently extended my hand with the biscuit again. Dixie backed away again.

"Mommy! I'm stuck!"

I grabbed the tops of Kimmy's boots, which were embedded in a pool of oozy mud, and yanked them and my obstinate daughter into my arms. Dixie's head popped around an uprooted tree no more than an arm's length away. She whined.

"Mommy! Look!"

There in the cavity the roots had made were Dixie's puppies and Kimmy's Winnie-the-Pooh. I looked up and saw the overhanging branches of the nearby oak tree. They had made a protective cover for Dixie from last night's rain. Dixie's puppies wiggled contently in their dry bed. She had protected her offspring and guided us to their whereabouts. It was as if she'd thought it through, just how she would present her little bundles of joy.

I looked at these twelve wiggly black-and-white puppies. I remembered the Bible verse I had read last night: "Are not two sparrows sold for a copper coin? And not one of them falls to the ground apart from your Father's will. But the very

> *People don't realize you have to stroke animals, not pet them. They don't like to be petted. You have to stroke them the way a mother's tongue licks them.*[5]
> Temple Grandin

hairs of your head are all numbered. Do not fear therefore; you are of more value than many sparrows" (Matt. 10:29–31 NKJV). "Someday I'll be a good mommy like Dixie," said Kimmy, "only I'm going to have a husband to help me." Kimmy shook her small head. "This is too much for just a mommy to take care of—"

The puppies whimpered in the background and Dixie licked Kimmy's cheek. I smiled, thinking, *Dixie has given my daughter her first life lesson in caring.* . . .

Only years later would I realize that Dixie's life lesson was meant for me too. You just never know. I never dreamed I would be the president of an interchurch women's group in our neighborhood, or that an endorsement to support the crisis pregnancy center would arise. But God knew.

My daughter outdid me. Married and with two little boys of her own, Kimberly is a counselor for the Oxford Crisis Pregnancy Center.

It's been almost thirty years now, and Dixie and her Winnie-the-Pooh puppies are still fondly remembered. You just never know how God will intertwine his blessings into the fabric of our lives.

A Dinah by Any Other Name

Lorilee Craker

A Dog Named Sarah?

Eight years ago, when we adopted a one-year-old basset hound, the first thing I did was change her name. I mean, *Sarah*? I could name four or five human Sarahs right off the top of my head, and there's no way, with all my pent-up name passion, I was calling the dog Sarah. At the time I was writing my first baby name book, *A Is for Adam: Biblical Baby Names*, so the hound was definitely getting a biblical namesake.

We eventually chose Dinah because of its similarity to Sarah, and also because I just liked the jazzy, bluesy feel, à la Dinah Washington. I didn't know a single person named Dinah, and it seemed to suit a hound dog's vibe, sitting on the front porch, baying at the moon. Dinah Blue she was henceforth.

Since then I've become fascinated with the naming process pet owners go through when that wriggly puff of fur is laid in its alpha mommy and daddy arms for the first time. Beyond Max and Sam, Molly and Sadie (the top two dog names in the country for each gender), definite trends emerge when people name pooches. Some folks pick a canine ID from something that means a lot to them, some life experience, hero, or hobby. Others choose pined-for "human" names, something they wanted to call a baby but didn't for some reason. And then there's the group that flat-out name their dogs after someone they know, a risky proposition yet a surprisingly popular one.

My favorite category? Names that make me snicker. My friend's aunt (speaking of pent up) named her dog a naughty word just so she could say it over and over again and get it out of her system. Okay, so that's a bit subversive, but what about calling a teacup poodle with pink nails Brutus or Bubba, or a brawny pit bull Cupcake or Croissant? Wouldn't that be a perpetual knee-slapper? Although Traci's neighbors probably weren't slapping their knees when they heard her calling for Help. "It's so funny, when I call him all the neighbors come running," she said. "My brother had a dog named Taxi—same effect."

M Is for Meaningful—and Majerle

Some bipeds want to stamp something meaningful on their quadruped's heart-shaped tag. Take Ken and his family. Formerly missionaries

in Africa, they have picked the perfect name for their fluffy friend: Huyu Ni Mbwa Kubwa, which Ken said is Swahili for "That's a big dog." "We call him Mbwa (dog) for short."

Lori's husband is a pilot, and the whole family went airborne over their clever and significant doggie designation. "Our dog's name is Pancho Barnes—after the female barnstormer pilot. She was the same era as Amelia Earhart, but we thought it might be a bit of a mouthful to keep saying, 'Come, Amelia. Sit, Amelia. Stay, Amelia.'"

Often a sports or literary hero carries great weight in a family's lore. Full of admiration for a great hoops star, Michele and her family couldn't help but bestow his last name on their German shepherd. "We named our dog Majerle (pronounced 'Marley') after former professional basketball player Dan Majerle of the Phoenix Suns and Central Michigan University," she said. "His middle name is Abraham, as our six-year-old had learned about Abraham that day in Sunday school and loved the story! And now someone had to go and write *Marley and Me*, so now our name is not that original."

(Majerle Abraham? It beats the pants off Buddy and Champ in the originality department, Michele!)

Pined-for Human Names

Let's say you have chosen a handful of baby names that, for whatever subjective reason, make your heart beat a little faster. Hypothetically, you have three beloved girl names in this big, wide world, and you only have two girls. What on earth do you do with the name that didn't make the "human cut"? In one woman's case, shaggy Shelly became the "daughter" she never had.

"My mom always wanted a daughter named Michelle," says Dan. "She hoped for four girls and got four boys instead, so she decided to name our first dog (a female) Shelly, short for Michelle." But, as Dan's story illustrates, this method of assigning a cherished yet ubiquitous name to a four-legged creature can backfire.

"The Avon lady came to the door one time, a-knocking away, and the dog was barking, so my mom kept yelling, 'Shelly! Shut your mouth!' The Avon lady seemed quite taken aback, since it turned out her name was Shelley."

Puppy Love

My teenage nephew named his puppy Ashley in a fit of adolescent crushing on a certain thirteen-year-old girl in his youth group. Of course, Ashley the human went on to grind that love-struck boy under her heel like a wad of gum a couple of years later—more than once, actually. And the poor kid's stuck with a huge, black, drooling namesake to remind him of his folly.

Some tribute names make a bit more sense, although it will depend on the honoree as to whether or not dubbing a dog in their honor is welcomed. Mary Carol's father-in-law for one was tickled. "Once it became obvious that we were not going to have another boy in our family, I called Dad and said, 'We got a Jack Russell terrier puppy, and this is your last chance to have someone named after you.' He said, 'I'll take it!' So Bill the dog it is."

A Dinah by Any Other Name

Recently, I ran into Dinah's previous owner.

"How's Sarah doing?" she asked, as I scrolled through the list of Sarahs in my brain. "The dog. Aren't you the people we gave Sarah to?"

Oh, that *Sarah. As in, Dinah.*

I didn't get into the name change as I updated her on the rambunctious hound she had owned for just a few months before she decided her apartment was too small for a dog. Why didn't I tell her Sarah had padded through the last eight years of her life as Dinah Blue? Because I didn't have time, because I thought she might be mildly offended, and mostly, because just as baby naming is a privilege of parenthood, giving a beloved dog the perfect name, the moniker that suits both the dog and the family who loves it, is the inalienable right of pet ownership.

Besides, a dog by any other name wouldn't be our sweet, smelly, one-of-a-kind Dinah Blue.

The Money Dog—Worth Her Weight in Gold

Chrissy Drzewiecki

One very hot August day when I was a single mom, I was working in the office of a roofing company. My eighteen-year-old son worked with me. Next door to my workplace was the office of a general contractor in the construction field. This particular morning, my guys were out in the field, so the office was slow.

The general contractor's wife from next door came over to ask me to see something. I quickly walked over to their office, through the front reception area, and into a small back room. There stood a dog looking up at me with dark sad eyes. She had been given to the general contractor by a transient who lived along the railroad tracks behind our building. She was a black Labrador and border collie mix, the last of the litter. I squatted down in front of her and told her to sit. She sat. And then she looked up at me, and her eyes told me to take her home. I did.

My sixteen-year-old son had been pestering me for a dog he could call his own. Anyone with kids, teens or otherwise, knows that as a parent you will wind up caring for this must-have pet. Still, I could not resist.

The first day home, she swallowed a nickel, so we named her Money Dog. The following day when we got home from work, we discovered she had taken the bathroom tissue out of the bathroom. When we followed it around the hallway and into the living room, we found it encircled a bunch of other miscellaneous must-haves she had neatly placed in a pile. She just sat there, looking at us. Border collies round things up. How in the world could you be mad at that?

That's where it all began—our love for a puppy who needed us. A puppy we needed.

Both my boys were teenagers, and they needed a diversion. Money Dog gave that to them. They couldn't wait to get home from school to see what she had done, what they could teach her, and even what she could teach them. It was amazing to watch them with her, learning to nurture her and train her. They taught her to jump from couch to love seat to couch without touching the floor. And I allowed it. It kept them busy. No more "Mom, I'm bored!"

This dog turned their hearts and mind to mush. And yes, mine too. And we laughed. We had so many serious moments of work, discipline, homework, bills to pay, battles to win . . . or lose. Money Dog gave us back our laughter and taught us how to have fun together.

We could not say the word *ride* too loudly or we would have to drop everything and take her for one, even if it was just around the block. It excited her so! Many weekends turned into field trips with Money Dog (and peace for me). She loved going for rides. There she sat, with her elbow on the arm of the car door, head out the window, fur blowing in the breeze, tongue hanging out. Quite the visual, isn't it? You didn't want to be in the backseat, that's for sure!

Off my boys and the dog would go, camping in their favorite spot where Money Dog loved rock climbing and jumping into the river to retrieve sticks bigger than she was, always wanting to please. Then they would get home, exhausted, and Money Dog would seek out our cat, Special K, and fall asleep. All was well in our world again.

She was such a loving, smart, compassionate dog. She loved all three of our cats. The last kitten we got was a stray who thought Money Dog was her mommy. Money Dog didn't care. She loved kids. She loved people—even the mail carriers. She

did raise a fuss when the local electric or gas company came to read the meters, though. Her hair would stand up on her back. I felt protected, and they didn't know she wouldn't hurt a fly.

She knew how to take only one or two treats out of the box. She would actually smile at us. And she didn't even mind when my youngest son shaved her fur off and made the shape of "M Dog" on her back. Unconditional love.

One of the most amazing memories I have is of the time my eighty-three-year-old mom came to visit us. It was a long journey for her, alone on a plane from Michigan to California. By now both my sons were out of the house. Mom was in the early stages of dementia, and she was feeling a bit over-whelmed. She still had such a sweet spirit and gentle soul, though—she laughed at anything and everything.

This uneventful day, Mom was sitting on the couch, pretty lethargic, just staring out the window. Suddenly, Money Dog walked up to her, sat at her feet, put her paw on her leg, and looked up at her with dark eyes as if to say, "Cheer up! I'm pretty bored too." Mom put a huge smile on her face and began to pet Money Dog. The dog laid her face on Mom's leg. Both of them were as content as can be. It was fabulous to see how our wonderful, compassionate dog knew Mom needed that affection right at that time.

I believe it is God's perfect timing to do just the right thing at just the right time for those he loves. My sons needed Money Dog. So did Mom. So did I.

God is good—he knows what we need when we need it. And for that I will always be thankful.

A New Calling

Sherri Gallagher

I want a German shepherd." I kept my head tipped down to hide my tears and pretended to scrub at a stubborn spot on a dish. Our last Afghan hound, Khan, had died, and we were dogless.

My husband, Jim, leaned against the kitchen doorjamb and watched for a few moments. Quietly he walked up behind me. He reached out with his right hand and shut off the faucet. Gently he wrapped both arms around me and rested his chin on my head. "You don't want another Afghan hound? We can afford a good one this time."

It was true. But while we had the cash flow to purchase expensive breed stock and now owned the facilities to house them, the time to make it work didn't exist. It took both our salaries to pay the mortgage, car payment, day care, and myriad other expenses of day-to-day living. We were both working seventy-hour weeks and now had a four-year-old to think about. In the long run, our son would have more opportunities and we would have a secure retirement. In the short run, life was a demanding grind to be endured, and pleasures like showing dogs were unrealistic dreams.

"I want a dog I can have outside with Shane and know it'll keep him safe, not one he has to watch and keep out of the road." I turned and buried my face in Jim's chest, hugging him to relieve the pain of losing Khan. I'm not sure what got his shirt soggier, my tears or my wet hands.

"Get what you think is best. You know shepherds."

The next day I looked through the local paper and found an ad for a German shepherd puppy. I deliberately arrived early for our appointment to make sure the facilities hadn't been spruced up to impress a potential buyer. Three months old and the last of the litter, the puppy had a kennel run all to herself. The facility was spotless. The parents' bloodlines were good with excellent hips and no inbreeding. More importantly, the parent dogs were there on-site, clean, healthy, and polite. I paid the fee and loaded the puppy into my car for the short trip home.

Shane's eyes shone. He immediately took to being tumbled and covered in puppy kisses. Jim took one look at the fur-covered tornado and named her Tasmanian Devil—Taz for short.

Taz had a lot more drive than I remembered my parents' shepherds having. Certainly she had better lungs. The first week we left her in the kitchen when we went to bed. She whimpered and howled all night. My husband evicted the dog to the kennel, and she immediately slept through the hours of darkness. Turns out she didn't want to be a house dog.

Taz grew into a pretty, eighty-five-pound, black-and-tan girl. She never slowed down. One spring day when Shane was six, he and the dog were outside playing. He came through the door with his face, stomach, and pants coated in brown, slimy mud. His facial expression resembled some tribal masks I'd seen in Hawaii, with scrunched-up eyes and an open, down-turned mouth. His words were incoherent. He released a deep huff, turned, and stomped away. That's when we understood the problem. There were muddy paw prints up his back. Taz must have mowed him face-first into a puddle like the characters in a Roadrunner cartoon.

I continued to travel for work, which sounds glamorous but actually ranked slightly above getting hit by a truck on the fun meter. At one airport I found a book titled *So That Others May Live* by Caroline Hebard. It was the autobiography of a woman who became involved in canine search and rescue. Shane loved to have nonfiction dog stories read to him at bedtime, and this book was perfect. In it, the author outlined just what she looked for in a search dog. It fit our Tasmanian Devil to a tee. My fingers itched to write for information, but how could I do search and rescue on top of everything else?

The next trip hit my breaking point. I unlocked my office door when my boss's assistant signaled for me to come to the president's office.

"You're leaving tonight with a customer to qualify a mold in Germany," my boss said. "You have a 6:00 p.m. flight. Make sure the customer is happy." He shuffled some papers and glanced up at me as if my continued presence annoyed him.

"I need more notice than this. My husband is out of town, and I don't have anyone to watch my son."

"Sounds like a personal problem. Be on the plane or don't come in tomorrow." He turned away from me and picked up his telephone.

I glanced at the ticket receipt and turned back to his assistant. "How long has the boss known he was sending me on this trip?"

"I don't know for sure, but he had me get the ticket last week," she said.

When I got back from Germany, I found a new job with less money, less travel, and the understanding that my son ranked higher than a "personal problem."

I found the search and rescue book tucked under Shane's bed. I wrote to the address in the back of the book, and they put me in contact with the closest search and rescue team, seventy miles south of me. It wasn't long before Taz and I were making almost weekly treks to learn how to man-trail.

The team encouraged me to start my own group, and after making the trip in an ice storm, I took their advice. Taz took to search and rescue (SAR) like a flea takes to fur. She wasn't fond of human remains work, but if I asked, she'd do it. Shane loved going out to hide for the dogs to find him. I think the dogs thought he was the most directionally challenged kid they ever met.

Other people joined us, and we applied to the American Rescue Dog Association (ARDA) to become one of their units. We took courses in first aid, map and compass, and radio training. Taz and I started to run together so we could meet the fitness requirement to run three miles in thirty minutes.

The ARDA people had drummed into my head that when I started training a SAR dog, I had to give her positive encouragement when she pointed out human scents. On one of our runs we went by a small private homeowners' association boat dock. As we passed the dumpster, the stench made me cough and gag. Taz did a skidding change of direction and

124

clearly had hit a human scent. She headed straight for the dumpster. Visions of finding a body filled my mind as I followed her. She blew past the dumpster, continuing toward the Porta John.

I breathed a mental sigh of relief. She didn't break stride at the potty but whipped around a tree, where she stopped and circled a fisherman relieving himself after a long morning (and I'm assuming a large thermos of coffee). I'm not sure if he understood my ecstatic, "Good girl. Good find."

Jim converted an old bread truck into a base camp. Maaco painted it white for free and a sign maker added our logo as a donation to the team. We had a lot of camping equipment, and Jim built shelves and counters inside the truck to hold everything. SAR was something we began to enjoy as a family.

When Shane was eleven, I picked him up from a sleepover (although I think very little sleeping was involved). By this time my young son was an expert at map and compass, so we gave him a location, and he took off with a tarp and a sleeping bag. I headed out with Taz and one of the base camp operators following me.

I had bronchitis that day. I got tired early and wanted to go home, so I called Shane on the radio. No response. I wasn't worried; Taz had my full trust. But the base camp operator panicked. He started hurrying up and down the trails, shouting and looking for Shane. Taz had slowed her pace to keep track of me, and she gave me a quizzical look when the man got out in front of her.

"Ignore him, Taz. Find Shane."

A short distance later she turned into the trees, pushed the leaves that had fallen on his brown tarp out of the way, and slipped inside to lick Shane awake.

After two years of training and preparation, we were ready. National evaluators came from New Jersey and Maryland to test our capabilities. Taz and I pulled the long multiple problem. We would be given a search with two subjects in an area so large we would need to work for a block of time between two to four hours. The test would be deliberately started late in the day so that the majority of it would be done in the dark.

The evaluators set up the problem, expecting me to take it easy on my eight-year-old dog and myself by working along the contours of the ridge instead of climbing up and down hills repeatedly. That wasn't our style. I checked the wind and sent Taz to work, heading up the first wooded incline. Fifteen minutes later we had both subjects.

The evaluators weren't going to let us scurry back to base camp and lounge in the relative warmth of a tent in winter. They told me to pretend we had a third subject and prove both my dog and I could keep working for long time periods. Taz and I tramped through a big patch of wild sage and bulldozed our way through brambles. After two hours we were two hills and almost half a mile from camp. The evaluators told me to take a heading back to base. Taz and I took off in a straight line. I would have danced my way back. I knew we'd passed, but the rough ground and heavy vegetation limited me to the occasional skip. Taz read my mood and raced circles around me all the way back. We were approved to take searches.

My first real search came a few months later when Taz located a drowning victim. The first day they put us out on an airboat into the open section of water. Taz identified the gloves of the missing man. When we hauled them into the boat, she cringed, tucking her tail and head and giving me the saddest look. It was her natural response to the scent of death.

126

The next day we worked on the ten-inch-thick ice surrounding the open water. At a pressure crack, Taz alerted. Other dogs were brought in, but no one could confirm her find. Several days later, underwater camera crews located the man fifteen feet from where Taz alerted and almost two hundred yards from where everyone expected to find the body.

Another time a fireman called us to find two CPR dummies in the fireproof gear he had lost during a rescue diver training. In the space of two hours, Taz found both dummies, the back half of a car someone had dumped in the lake, and a flipper one of the divers had lost. That convinced the fire chief to use dogs on water searches.

When the towers came down on September 11, many of my friends and their dogs responded. I didn't go. The smell of death saturated the air. I knew it would stress Taz permanently, and I couldn't ask that of her.

Taz was always there—my go-to girl. At ten she developed a brain tumor and became blind. Her replacement, Clara, had to step up and fill some pretty big paw prints. Even so, I would put down tracks for Taz in the backyard so she could do the work she loved. She had so much fun searching, there could have been a hundred sites to spread her ashes. I settled for scattering them among my rosebushes and lavender where she had chased Clara and rolled to her heart's content.

While dogs have saved my life and sanity on more than one occasion, only one changed it completely—Tasmanian Devil. She led me to understand the road God had spent almost forty years preparing me to take. As long as a canine search and rescue unit exists, a little piece of Taz will always be around, working so others may live.

Jack and Willa—A Love Story

Alison Hodgson

When I first considered getting a dog, I read every book I could get my hands on and talked to every dog owner I ran into. My children, deprived of their own dogs, were in the habit of cozying up to dogs wherever they could: parks, garage sales, the sidewalk in front of our house (dog owners in a hurry learned to avoid our street), anywhere really. So I was able to conduct many interviews during this research phase. While my children made their moves on the dogs, I chatted up the owners. One of the questions I always asked was, "How did you choose your dog?"

The answers were varied. A lot of people said, "He/She chose me!" I'd done enough reading to suspect that their dogs were simply dominant. Many tried to match their dog to their lifestyle: active owners tried to choose high-energy dogs and less active owners tried to select more sedentary ones. Some of the dog owners had a family member with allergies to consider. Some had always admired a particular breed. Many had simply gone to a shelter and fallen in love; I heard that a lot.

In all my conversations I never heard anyone say that they chose a dog because of an unborn child, but I did just that, and this baby hadn't even been conceived except in the minds of God and her parents . . . and me. I'm referring to my niece, Willa.

When I first began all this reading and talking about dogs, I really wasn't sure a dog was a good idea for our family. In the beginning I ruled out many breeds because my youngest daughter, Eden, was only a baby. I paid attention to the guidelines established by rescue organizations, and if they wouldn't place their dogs in families with babies and very young children, no matter how attracted I was to a particular breed, I no longer considered it.

Years passed, Eden grew, and I began to reevaluate some of the rejected but much-admired breeds. Then my sister Torey reminded me that she was hoping to have another baby.

Torey and her family are frequent visitors. For her daughter Ren, who is six months younger than Eden, our home is a quasi–Disney World with a bit of heaven thrown in. Frequently Torey awakens to a little face inches from her own and the question, "EmIgonnagotomuhcousins'housetoday?" Torey suspected the love affair would extend to any of her future children, and she didn't want her theoretical baby being attacked by my theoretical dog. I saw her point and went back to keeping the same standards I had been using as I searched for a dog.

By the time we brought Jack the dog home, our son, Christopher, was eleven, our older daughter, Lydia, was nine, Eden was four, and their cousin Ren was three and a half. A month later Torey became pregnant with Willa.

The day of Willa's birth, Jack knew something was strange. When we returned from the hospital that night, he ran around smelling each one of us thoroughly. The next day I brought home a little knitted hat Willa had worn, like all the dog books recommended, as if she was our own baby. When Willa herself finally visited, we carefully introduced her to Jack. He was excited to meet that thing he had smelled, but when we cautioned him to be gentle, he quickly calmed down.

Every time Willa came to visit, Jack made a stop at her car seat for a sniff, sometimes greeting her with a gentle lick on the foot. Frequently we found him sleeping on the ground beside her car seat.

At first Willa was oblivious to all this devotion, but as she became more alert, she was very interested in Jack. We showed her how to pet him. Since she didn't have much motor control, petting translated to a gentle whacking that Jack tolerated. Torey brought a blanket to put on the carpet in a vain attempt to keep Willa from being coated in black fur. Jack considered this an invitation to plop down too. After I ruled that out, he contented himself with stretching out as close to an edge as he could come without actually touching the blanket. Sometimes he would drag a towel from his kennel and rest his head on that.

Although Jack was very gentle with Willa, Torey and I never left them alone. We were both there the first time Jack saw Willa crawling. It spooked him. He scuttled back, startled, and then ran into the kitchen where he sprinted around the island several times.

For the next several weeks, every time he saw Willa, Jack went running in the other direction and refused to come anywhere near her. Torey and I laughed about it, imagining what he could be thinking. From her birth we had pretended that he called her "the Thing" and "Thingie." One of us would speak for him in a dopey voice, "I don't know what you're doing, Thingie. Just stay back!"

So the only time Jack was willing to be near Willa was when she was restrained in her high chair. Jack had quickly realized that whenever Willa ate a meal, he had a snack. He posted himself just to the right of the high chair, sitting at attention, looking regal and handsome.

It wasn't long before Willa understood why Jack was there and began to drop food on purpose. The second anything hit the ground, Jack scrapped his stately pose and scuttled like a rat to snatch it. This sharing had not been forbidden, but they both knew it should be kept on the down low. When someone walked by, Willa slyly pulled her hand back while Jack casually looked away. Torey and I had fun talking for Jack: "Oh Thingie, keep the good stuff coming!"

Other than these mealtime truces, Jack remained skittish when Willa was loose until I decided to force a complete détente. I laid down a big quilt on the living room floor and emptied a basket of Willa's toys on it. Torey set her down amidst them. Jack watched this from across the room. Next I scattered a few of his toys around, patted the blanket, and called his name.

This was an offer Jack couldn't refuse. Settling on the edge of the blanket, he rested his head on his big paws and warily eyed Willa. She was happy with a toy but dropped it the second she noticed Jack and scrabbled across the quilt to pet him. He stiffened as if awaiting a blow. My daughter Lydia picked up Willa and helped her to gently pet while

I leaned against Jack, petting him and speaking softly. He began to relax and was soon on his side, nearly asleep, with Willa nestled against his belly.

From there the love only grew, and it's a good thing. It wasn't long before Willa was walking and talking, toddling after Jack wherever he went and calling, "Ja! Ja!" This made us all laugh since she rarely said "Mama," and as of this writing I'm still waiting for her to say my name.

Once Willa was fussing as Torey strapped her into the car seat. "Do you want to go see Aunt Ali?" Torey asked as a distraction. Willa sat up and grunted in apparent affirmation.

"Do you want to see Jack?" Torey asked.

"Yesh! Yesh! Yesh!" Willa shouted.

Later that day Willa and Jack had a collision near the back door. He had been following her closely and when she stopped short, he didn't. I heard Willa's upset shout and was ready to intervene when I saw her raise one little hand. Jack immediately hit the down position and sat, eyes intent on her. She threw him a Cheerio that he caught in the air. She resumed her drunken toddle, and he continued to follow, maintaining a more respectful distance.

Years ago when Jack was just a thought and Willa was only a dream, if you had asked me, "What are you looking for in a dog?" I wouldn't have been able to answer you succinctly. I probably would have gone on about breeds and behaviors, tendencies and temperaments. I almost certainly would have mentioned fur.

But if you had shown me a picture of the future moment that Jack, though four times her size, sat submissively before Willa, I would have said, "This. I want this."

TLC for the OES

Judythe Morgan

I have two dogs, a large Old English sheepdog (a breed commonly called OES) named Micah and a mixed-breed rescue dog named Bernie. I didn't need another dog. My husband didn't want another dog. Yet when a friend called to say her neighbor needed a home for Rhinestone, their two-year-old OES, I couldn't stop myself from going to see her dog.

After convincing my husband that we should at least have a look at Rhinestone, we went to see why she needed a new home. What we heard was a sad and often-repeated story with our beloved breed. Those looking for a puppy see the small black-and-white creature, all fluffy and playful, an adorable panda bear, and they simply fall in love. Who wouldn't?

Rhinestone's owners hadn't stopped to think that the cute little puppy would grow into a large, seventy-pound dog that would crave attention and need constant grooming and care. Instead, Rhinestone had lived outside, isolated and neglected. With no socialization, she had become a wild thing. She needed lots of TLC and training.

We recognized the commitment we'd be making, and although I promised to shoulder most of the burden, I couldn't convince my husband. Practically, I knew he was right. We did already have two dogs. We suggested the owners call the OES rescue in town.

As we were leaving, Rhinestone came to the edge of the fence. She was such a mess, with her hair all matted and unshaped, that only an OES breed lover would recognize her as a sheepdog. Her big pink tongue panted in the Texas heat. Her beautiful brown eyes locked with mine. That sad little face blurred as tears filled my eyes. My heart weighed heavily in my chest. I prayed she'd find a good home.

Weeks passed. We assumed Rhinestone had been placed in a rescue home until my friend called again. Her neighbor had called the county animal control to pick up Rhinestone. My heart jumped to my throat. That couldn't happen. She'd end up at the shelter, unadoptable, and ultimately would be put down. I told my friend to stop the dogcatcher. I immediately called my husband at work and then the owner, who agreed to give us time to pick up Rhinestone. She even agreed to pay the vet bills to have her spayed.

Rhinestone remembered me from our connection on the first visit. She came toward me, spotted the leash in my hand, then turned and ran. Had someone beaten her too? She raced around the yard, afraid to come near us. My husband finally tackled her then lifted her into the kennel in our car.

Poor Rhinestone, who had never been confined before, thrashed around. I sat beside the crate, my fingers poking through the wire, and cooed soft words to her all the way to our veterinarian. We had to find someone to love her. Someone who would give her a forever home.

Our vet took one look at the matted mess of a dog and shook his head. "What have you taken on?"

I handed him Rhinestone's veterinary records we'd gotten from the owner as I explained the situation. "I couldn't let her go to the pound," I said as his assistant took her to be examined.

He nodded his understanding. "We'll clean her up. Probably have to shave her down to be sure there's no mange or flea infestation. Then get her up-to-date on immunizations. She's had no shots since her puppy immunizations. I'll call you, but I'm thinking we'll keep her overnight."

"That's fine. She's had a rough time. We want her to be taken care of," my husband said. With all the dirt on his shirt, the poor man looked like he'd been mud wrestling. He even had a scratch on his cheek from Rhinestone's too-long nails.

I'd like to say that Rhinestone came home from the vet a new dog. She didn't. She was clean and healthy looking but not at all sure what to do in her new situation with regular meals, daily walks, and two new friends. She did gradually calm down. She'd never been an inside dog but quickly took to the new routine, copying Micah and Bernie. The boys

---

Let There Be Peace on Earth, and Let It Begin with Dogs . . .

There's a remarkable lack of conflict in dog packs. That's because members resolve the situation when disagreements arise, then move on. Imagine what our world would be like if we dealt with our conflicts before they escalated out of control.[6]

Cesar Millan, the Dog Whisperer

accepted this new addition to the pack without protest. It was like they wanted to help her too.

Rhinestone wouldn't have much to do with my husband. After all, he'd tackled her. She jumped every time he made a sudden move. She obeyed him fine, but as long as she lived with us, she never truly warmed up to him. As for me, well, Rhinestone became my best friend. She slept on the floor beside my bed, followed me into my dressing room closet and around the house as I did my chores, and napped at my feet as I wrote at my computer. She wanted me close by.

If she couldn't see me, she wanted to be with my sister-in-law Keta, who was living with us temporarily. Something instantly clicked between Rhinestone and Keta. With me, Rhinestone knew she had a protector and provider. But with Keta, Rhinestone found another lonely soul.

When Keta moved into her small apartment a few weeks later, we offered to let her take Rhinestone. She said no. The apartment was small and had no yard for a large dog. Of course, by this time Rhinestone had decided she loved being a house dog and rarely went outside except for walks. For some unspoken reason, Keta didn't want to take Rhinestone. I didn't insist. At her age, Keta knew what she could handle, and truthfully, I wasn't ready to give up my girl.

After a month in her new apartment, Keta decided she missed having a companion. Her dog had died before she moved in with us, and she'd just spent months in a house with three dogs. She was feeling lonely so she got a cat, thinking that a cat in the apartment would be best. A dog lover at heart, that didn't work at all. We moved the cat to live in the barn at a friend's ranch.

Over the next few months, Keta lost her zeal. She put on a good front, but when you caught her in unguarded moments, you could see sadness in her eyes. The same sadness I'd seen in Rhinestone's eyes that first day.

As hard as it was for me to think about not having Rhinestone around, I knew Keta needed Rhinestone. My husband and I booked a month's vacation at a place with a two-pet limit. We could only take Micah and Bernie. We asked Keta to board Rhinestone at her place.

When we returned, the change in both Keta and Rhinestone was phenomenal. Their time together had made their bond even stronger, but Keta insisted she couldn't take our dog from us.

"Okay," I said. "But could you just keep her a little while longer? We've scheduled some remodeling projects. All the male workers in the house will stress Rhinestone too much.

I think she'd be happier here." That was the truth, not just an argument to give the dog and my sister-in-law more time together. Rhinestone didn't single out my husband in her wariness. All males frightened her.

Rhinestone stayed with Keta as complication after complication extended our remodeling projects. I frequently escaped the pounding of hammers and grinding of saws at Keta's apartment.

One day as we shared a cup of tea with Rhinestone at our feet, Keta said, "I think she likes it here just fine."

"I think she should stay here forever." My sister-in-law looked shocked. I nodded. "I do. After all, I can visit her every day if I want to, and it's not like I don't have Micah and Bernie."

My sister-in-law's eyes glazed with tears. "You'd let her stay here permanently with me?"

Reaching across the table, I squeezed Keta's hand and then looked down at Rhinestone. The sweet dog dipped her head as if to say thank you, then rested her nose on Keta's foot. "Of course. I truly believe that's the reason God brought Rhinestone to us in the first place . . . so you two could keep each other company."

In our home, Rhinestone would always be one of the pack. Loved and cherished, but still one of three. With Keta, she was the only dog . . . the one who cared for another lonely soul. I knew she'd found her forever home.

Three-Legged Sentinel

Roberta Hupprich

*F*arai, my new friend, was adamant. "You must have a guard dog."

"But why? We don't have anything worth stealing."

She leaned forward to make her point. "You have a computer, yeah, and a TV? That's what thieves want—electronics." Taking a deep breath, then exhaling, Farai leaned back against the wall and waited for my response.

I wrinkled up my nose and answered, "We already have an alarm system, an electric fence on top of a six-foot wall, and burglar bars on the windows! What else do we need?"

"I tell you—a guard dog. This is Zimbabwe."

My husband, Glenn, and I were missionaries with the Methodist church. I was a nurse working with street children and orphans while Glenn was responsible for allocating donations to the designated mission projects. We arrived in Zimbabwe by way of Zambia, where we had lived for one year after being evacuated from the Democratic Republic of

139

Congo (Zaire). Thanks to a change in regimes, our time in the Congo had been somewhat turbulent.

But now we were looking forward to a less stressful assignment where we could lay our heads down at night and feel reasonably safe. No gunshots, no house searches, and definitely no guard—man or dog. So on the appointed day we stuffed our belongings in the back of our Cruiser, bid our missionary colleagues good-bye, and headed south, looking forward to a new challenge.

Did we really need a dog? Farai's words echoed in my head, "You must have a guard dog." I threw up my hands in surrender and reverted to the one thing I knew held true—when in doubt in Africa, trust the African. So Glenn and I made the rounds of pet adoption agencies in Harare until we finally found the right dog.

His name was Rex, a royal name befitting a German shepherd. He had been hit by a car at the tender age of six months, resulting in the loss of a back leg. His owner gave him up to the Society for the Prevention of Cruelty to Animals. We adopted Rex because he had a thunderous bark and fierce-looking teeth. Thieves would never notice he had only three legs.

But for me, it was the way he wagged his tail with such vigor that his back leg swiveled side to side. Glenn called him Tripod. I kept my fingers crossed, hoping Rex—or Tripod—would meet with Farai's approval.

Farai shook her head and chuckled. "What's he gonna do, beat 'em to death with his tail?"

Rex was happy most of the time, with one exception. He was afraid of thunder. We knew a storm was coming long before it happened. Trembling with fear, our guard dog would abandon his house in the backyard and cower behind the woodpile on our verandah where we often sat to catch a cool breeze. Looking pitiful, he would beg for mercy with his large brown eyes. "Maybe we should let him in," I would suggest, "at least until it stops thundering." Shrugging his shoulders, Glenn always agreed.

As the economy in Zimbabwe declined, Glenn's work became more difficult. The children's home being built with donated funds from churches in the United States was in jeopardy. The cost of cement, when it was even available, soared from $3 a sack in 2000 to $15 a sack by 2006. The number of AIDS orphans continued to rise, breaking the back of government social services. The weight of seeing my AIDS patients beginning to die, due in part to the lack of nutritious foods, was painful. I didn't know how to fix it. The blessings that kept me strong were slowly being overshadowed by tragedy. Children were going to school with nothing in their stomachs. If they were lucky, they carried a sweet potato tucked in their book bag for lunch.

I often arrived home at the end of the day feeling defeated and angry. Rex always met me with an enthusiastic greeting when I stepped out of the vehicle. Sometimes I would push him away, not wanting to be bothered, but he always came back.

His love was unconditional. Surrendering to the persistent pokes with his snout, I would greet him with a perfunctory pat on the head, saying, "What a good boy." Before I knew it, I had a smile on my face and the load I was carrying seemed lighter. Little by little Rex was becoming a member of our family, no longer just a guard dog.

When 2006 arrived, it was time for us to leave Africa and return home to retire. Finding a home for Rex was not going to be easy. One very cold night during the dry season, while warming ourselves in front of the fireplace, Glenn raised the question that had been on both our minds: "What do we do about Rex? He eats too much, and who wants a three-legged guard dog anyway, besides us? Mohamed [a Zimbabwean associate] was in the office today. At first he said he would take Rex, but then when I told him the dog only had three legs, he laughed and said, 'Oh no! I want a real dog.'"

"It's for the best," I said, chewing on my thumbnail. Neither of us could envision Rex as a vicious guard dog, and the thought of having him put down, which had been suggested, sickened me.

In March, two months prior to leaving Zimbabwe, we had no takers for Rex. Still stinging from the astronomical quote for shipping our "free" dog home, I began walking Rex on a leash and bringing him in at night to get him ready for life in Florida. Running free was no longer an option. The retirement community we were going to had a leash law.

These were desperate times for all Zimbabweans. It was not uncommon for the electricity in Harare to go off. Occasionally thieves would steal copper wiring or electrical components from a relay box, or cut the wires to deactivate alarm systems in a neighborhood before a rash of break-ins.

At three o'clock one morning, Rex began barking and running back and forth in the hall to get our attention. His thunderous bark echoed off the high ceiling and bare walls. Half asleep, Glenn yelled out, "Rex, quiet down. You sound like a pack of vicious dogs for heaven's sake."

Since Rex did not quiet down, we dragged ourselves out of bed to see what the problem was. As our eyes adjusted to the darkness, we realized our electricity had been cut. Our outside security light no longer shone through our bedroom drapes to bathe the room in translucent light. It was pitch-black.

Moving toward the living room window while slipping on my robe, I cautiously peeked out. "Maybe someone's in trouble and knocking on the gate." I didn't hear a sound.

Using a flashlight, Glenn found the broken dining room window with the burglar bars cut. "We've been robbed!" he shouted.

After shining their flashlight down the hall and catching sight of Rex's eyes and teeth in its beam, the intruders had scurried back out the same way they came in.

Soon after, Rex stopped barking but remained somewhat agitated. Reaching down to cup his head in my hands, I looked him in the eyes and said, "Good dog. Good dog, Rex. It's okay." Immediately he calmed down, and so did I.

Glenn checked the rooms to see what was missing. "Was your cell phone charging on the kitchen table?"

"Yeah."

"Well, they took it."

"Good. I hate those things." He was not pleased with my stab at levity.

Glenn shuddered when he spotted a brick laying on the kitchen floor where it was dropped by one of the thieves during his hasty retreat. It had been intended for our heads if we should wake up. What a close call.

Our house phone worked. Glenn called the police who said, "We have no transportation, but if you pick us up in the morning, we'll come out to take a statement and look over the place." Since there was nothing more to be done, we hugged Rex again, told him he was a good boy, and headed back to bed to wait for daybreak, though sleep did not come. The scene played over and over in our heads.

In the morning a police officer came. After going over the story, the officer looked down at Rex then back to us. "You're very lucky. That dog saved your life. These guys work in small groups. One waits outside the window to receive the goods while the others search the house room by room for electronics and jewelry."

How could we leave Rex behind? After all, he saved our lives. He was coming home with us despite the cost, and we were happy to pay.

Rex has taken well to retirement, having many two- and four-legged friends. Neighbors bring gifts of bones and biscuits, marveling at how well he runs on three legs when he spots a squirrel. We have learned not to place our coffee on the coffee table to avoid having it knocked off by his ever-wagging tail. Glenn still refers to him as Tripod. As for me, I'll stick with Rex, king of our castle and loving friend.

Respect

Paul Ingram

Peggy wasn't my dog. She made that clear from our first meeting. She was my friend and sometimes my companion, when she could fit me in around what she saw as her responsibilities. That was good enough for both of us as we ran free together in the far pasture. Ours was a different kind of friendship, not the sort of trusting connection that often exists between human and dog. But in a strange way, it worked, and it taught a little boy what respect is all about.

Since she came to us partly grown, an English shepherd mixed with some uncertain breed, Grandfather figured that Peggy must have been teased by children and fear became imprinted on her psyche. She was skittish even around Grandfather. I don't recall that he often, if ever, was allowed to scratch her ears or pet her white coat with dark brown splotches. In current terminology, Peggy needed her space. A no-man's zone always existed about a foot around her body. When it came to children like me, the zone extended out to two feet.

If anyone crossed a boundary, she turned toward the threat and immediately went into her snarling demon routine. It was impressive and fearsome. We all got the message and let her go her own way.

A working farm dog, Peggy was always ready for a romp with my grandfather and was especially adept at helping herd steers in the right direction. That isn't to say she was a master herder who didn't sometimes send her charges fleeing in the wrong direction. Given her personality, I think Peggy had a low threshold of patience and didn't suffer fools gladly, be they two-footed or four-hoofed. If animals weren't cooperating, she let fly with both barrels. She would watch to see which way we were trying to get the cattle to go, then she would jump in with four paws, running behind and nipping at the heels of the dawdlers.

This sounds easier than it was in practice. Peggy showed real artistry in rushing a heifer, nipping a little at the hind legs, and then dodging the kicks that were sure to follow. Only once did I ever see Peggy miss on her timing and take a hoof right in the nose. She yelped, sitting back on her haunches to get her bearings. Then Peggy looked around to see if anyone had noticed her embarrassing gaffe. After collecting her thoughts, she trotted back to work but stayed close to Grandfather. The fight had been knocked out of her for that day.

Peggy was a good ratter, always a valuable commodity on the old-time, general-purpose farms, which had barns and outbuildings that rodents loved. One day when I was about five years old, I was throwing sticks for Peggy to bring back. She suddenly became sidetracked by something in the grass nearby, and pounced on a tuft, digging furiously. Then she dropped that spot, jumped over a few feet, and the earth flew once more. At the third hole she hit paydirt and came up with a mole. It was obviously a day of triumph as she sat back with her tongue lolling, trying to catch her breath.

I don't think Peggy ever actually bit anyone, so in retrospect her anger seems to have been more of a self-protective show. I remained circumspect in respecting the rules, not willing to test her resolve. As long as I respected her, Peggy and I spent many happy, sunlit hours together. If no farm duties called, she shadowed my play and wanderings. She loved to roll in the snow, creating her own version of a snow angel.

There was a key to Peggy's heart. She was obsessed with the game of fetch. Whatever the object—stick, ball, bone—she would speed after it and return at a run. She would drop the object about two feet from the thrower and back up to allow access. Then she was ready to take off again, playing until the thrower's arm or attention span gave out. Now that I think of it, her companionship was a little self-serving. She hung around in hopes of a game.

Peggy taught me something about friendship. You take dogs—and people—as they come, quirks and all, accepting who they are and what they have been through that was hurtful. Since the days of my childhood, both I and my friends have tended to be of the quirky variety, often unlovely and even outcast. Perhaps it was Peggy who taught me how to love with respect.

A Saving Transformation

Chris Pedersen

*H*ow does a dog become the agent for a life-changing transformation? She wins your heart, that's how.

After a quick dinner one February evening, my husband, Bob, and I loaded Nur, our twelve-year-old son, and Hopper, our four-year-old golden retriever, into the SUV. Hopper had the privilege of sitting in the backseat for this special trip. Little did she know she was about to gain a companion.

It was Bob's idea to get another dog. I wasn't really keen on it—since I was the one staying home, it meant I'd have another dog to take care of. Bob thought we could breed the new dog and experience having puppies while our son was growing up. Oh boy! That was not a family experience I really wanted. "Are you sure?" I had said to Bob. What I really wanted to say was, "No." But that didn't fit my people-pleaser personality.

Bob had been an only child. He grew up on a small ranch with chickens, goats, and dogs, and as a teenager he raised sheep in 4-H. This provided him full participation in the cycle of life. He would say that his parents provided for all his emotional needs growing up, which imparted a confidence he carried into adulthood.

I, on the other hand, was the oldest of six kids and grew up in one of the many suburbs of Los Angeles. Small yards and close neighbors limited the practicality of having a dog. For a short time we had a boxer named Bija, but my father gave her away to a rancher who had lots of fenced area for her to roam. It hurt to see her go. Since Dad kept her chained to the garage, we had some comfort knowing she now had freedom. That was little comfort, however, compared to an understanding hug from Mom or Dad—something we never received in our home.

So this day with Nur and the dog, we drove to a breeder of Chesapeake Bay retrievers. He talked to us about the dogs' pedigree as we waded into the wiggly sea of cuddly puppies. They rolled around the enclosed area as we surveyed our choices. *How do we ever pick one out of all these adorable puppies?* I wondered.

"Let's look for one with a good wagging tail," said Nur. For a twelve-year-old, he was a thoughtful only child. His quest for a good tail-wagger led him to a runty, caramel-colored pup that showed interest in the legs wading through her space rather than in the other puppies.

"Look at this one's tail." Nur picked her up, and she licked him while her tail wagged nonstop. It was love at first lick.

We finished the purchase of our puppy and received a copy of her pedigree and AKC registration forms. "Hey! She was born on Christmas!" I declared, waving the registration form.

"That's so cool!" Nur responded as he snuggled her.

Hopper seemed indignant at the appearance of another dog in the vehicle. Her attitude was palpable as she snubbed the wiggly pup.

"What shall we name her?" I asked as we drove the thirty-minute trip home.

We tossed around several names and finally settled on Chessie. We later learned that all Chesapeake Bay retrievers were called Chessies. Oh well . . . When we sent in Chessie's AKC registration, we gave her the formal name Nur's Noel Chessie—a fine name for a dog with the same birthday as Jesus.

Chessie fit right into our family. Hopper being the demure type, as most goldens are, let Chessie take the top-dog position. And although she otherwise paid little attention to Chessie, Hopper initiated playtime and Chessie would happily oblige. She became a great companion for Hopper, bringing new life to a once lonely dog.

Chessie's tail became her signature. At any encounter it pounded the floor or wagged the air enthusiastically. It personified her smiley disposition. It displayed such vigor, we maneuvered to avoid it or else endured a good smack.

The three of us enjoyed the company of both dogs on many outings to lakes and hiking trails in the Sierras. We packed a lunch and made a day of it. Since we lived just a few miles from Folsom Lake, we often went for an hour or so to throw a stick or floating toy for the dogs. It amused us to watch Hopper fetch. Chessie would steal the object from her and then leave it behind. We called Chessie the broken retriever; she ran after a ball, picked it up, and left it before she returned to us.

"Bring it here, Chessie!"

"Go get the ball!"

She ignored the order as if it were a suggestion. We smiled. Of course it made us love her even more. How could we complain when she approached us with her typical enthusiasm, seeming to say, *Here I am, ready to love you. See my tail?*

Chessie and Hopper walked faithfully with me every weekday morning. Actually it was more like I walked faithfully with them. Their enthusiasm for a walk inspired me to keep exercising. Occasionally Deb, my friend and neighbor, walked with us.

One morning in early February as the light rose on an overcast day, Deb and I were walking with the dogs when a tragedy struck that began a journey of transformation for me. Who would have thought that a dog who made her way into my heart would become the catalyst for that transformation?

A speeding Porsche whizzed down the hill toward us, and before I could react, the car hit Chessie as she ran from the

And the Bark Goes On . . .

During the filming of the movie *Marley & Me*, the book's author, John Grogan, fell in love with one of the Labrador puppies on the set so much so that the producer gave him the little white puppy. Back home, Grogan discovered the dog had difficulty going upstairs. Turns out the little guy had severe hip dysplasia, common in Labs but not usually in one so young. Had the dog gone back to its breeder, it most likely would have been euthanized, leaving Grogan to conclude that this dog truly found its right home.

And that little guy wasn't alone. Twenty-two dogs played Marley on the set, trained by the same person who trained the dogs for the film *Hotel for Dogs*.

All the Marley dogs were adopted after filming by the crew, studio executives, and friends.[7]

field into the street. Now Chessie lay in the street. I felt scared as I hurried to her, terrified of knowing how badly she was hurt.

"I'll go get the car," Deb offered. Her house was close by.

Once Deb and her husband, Jim, arrived, we lifted Chessie into the back of the Suburban and I crawled in to be with her. We headed to the emergency veterinary hospital that was open that time of the morning.

I stroked Chessie's neck and whispered comforting words. My mind began to blur as I went over in my head the scene immediately preceding the accident. *Why didn't you wave down the Porsche driver? After all, the light was low and you knew she was out in the field. If only* . . . The thoughts haunted me as we pulled into the vet hospital's parking lot and transferred Chessie into their care.

We waited what seemed hours before Dr. Griffin, the orthopedic surgeon, called me into an exam room.

"She's doing fine and resting right now," he reported. "X-rays show her pelvis is broken, her front leg is fractured, and her heart is bruised. We'll do the surgery once her heart heals."

I shuddered at the words he spoke.

"She's very strong," encouraged the surgeon. "She'll get through this. Just don't expect that she'll be the same as before . . . running and playing."

His words were an answer to my unspoken question: *Could she survive and have a healthy life after all this?* Fortunately we could afford the cost of the surgery, so it never crossed my mind that she shouldn't have a chance at a full life.

I followed Dr. Griffin into another room to see Chessie. As we entered, we heard a loud pounding. *What was that sound?* Then I realized it was Chessie. She heard me and activated her signature greeting. Her tail pounded the floor of her stainless steel cage, amplifying the sound.

"How are you, sweet Chessie?" Even though she looked somber lying there in the confined space, her tail seemed to say she was happy.

Bob was in Southeast Asia on business when the accident occurred. The distance made our conversation that night difficult enough, but I did not expect it to be so troublesome.

"Just have them put her down."

"No, I can't do that!"

"She's just a dog, Chris," was his matter-of-fact reply. "If you'd lived on a ranch like I did, you'd know—you just put them down."

I heard plenty of stories from Bob about animals and the cycle of life. And when an animal was injured or got old, you would . . . well . . . you know. That was his experience.

"No!" I sobbed into the phone. "I won't let that happen to her."

The conversation went badly. But for the first time in my life I felt that I needed to be heard. Have a say. Get my way for a change.

This became a turning point in my life. It broke a pattern that began in my childhood and persisted into adulthood, a pattern resulting from an overcontrolling father. As children we had to be quiet and submissive. In addition, we endured psychological neglect due to lack of emotional support. As a result I developed a protective personality with a goal to please other people at all costs. This was not healthy behavior. It assured that my exterior reaction constantly masked my inner pain.

Making decisions for myself and speaking my mind were foreign experiences for me as I entered adulthood. I might have had an opinion about something but never felt compelled to take a stand . . . until now. I needed to stand up for Chessie.

I visited Chessie in the hospital while her heart healed. Bob and I continued to have strained conversations about it on the phone. By the time he returned from his trip, Chessie was through her surgery. We all visited Chessie regularly, and each time she showed her typical enthusiasm with a rhythmic pounding of her tail on the cage floor. During the visits, I began to see Bob's heart change toward her. He started to see the special dog I loved. How could you not love a dog that seemed to reach out and say, *I love you so much nothing else matters. Only you.*

On one visit, Dr. Griffin finally prepared us for taking Chessie home. He showed us a therapy cart they used to help dogs learn to walk following surgery. It looked like a three-dimensional box: a big frame on wheels formed out of PVC pipe and elbows with a body sling suspended from the frame top. Chessie needed a therapy cart to get better, and we had to build it.

We purchased all the pieces and spent the weekend constructing a therapy cart. I fabricated the body sling while Nur and Bob built the cart. Once completed, we were ready to bring Chessie home. We all went to pick her up—including Hopper.

Since Chessie's accident, Hopper had moped around looking sad and lonely. She did not understand what happened to her buddy Chessie. Compared to the first time we brought Chessie to the car while Hopper waited, she was anything but indignant; she expressed excitement at seeing her friend.

As prescribed, I worked with Chessie in the therapy cart to encourage her recovery. We kept the cart in the garage, and each time I got her into it, I opened the door so she could see outside.

It looked like rain one dreary morning in March when I lifted Chessie into the cart and opened the garage door. As the door went up, a light snow began to fall. It caught me by surprise. The quiet scene felt so peaceful. It seemed to awaken something in Chessie as she struggled in the cart sling.

"What are you doing, Chessie?"

She managed to free her front legs from the sling and was dragging the cart toward the open door. Amazed yet concerned for her, I freed her from the sling and cart and away she went. Moving at a pretty good pace, Chessie limped her way across the street to a field. What possessed her to suddenly begin walking I'll never know. But I knew for sure she was done with that therapy cart. Her fierce determination, energetic nature, and brute strength came through.

Chessie lived a happy and fulfilling life after the accident. She limped when she walked, never putting much pressure on that once fractured front leg. But throw a ball for her and she ran like the wind with no detectable disability. Most importantly she displayed her sweet, attentive nature that we loved so much. Her pounding, wagging tail continued to say *I love you.*

Bob came to realize that saving Chessie was worth the cost. She was priceless. We enjoyed the companionship of a dog who deserved a chance to live as she gave back so willingly and selflessly.

We discussed the transformation the experience brought to my life. It resulted in change that continued for years in both of our lives. Bob learned to listen to my new "voice," although it wasn't always welcome in the beginning. The transformation opened the way for healing other issues in our marriage. We began to uncover the differences in our upbringing, which led to understanding stress points in our relationship.

All this because one dog had wagged her tail into our lives and won our hearts. I will always remember Chessie. Time has passed and the tears have gone, but the memory of a very special dog, born on Christmas Day, lives on. In saving her life, I saved mine.

The Pound Puppy

Dorothy C. Snyder

*N*o, we do not want a dog!" I told my daughter. "I don't like dogs in the house, and besides, it would be too much additional work."

My daughter thought a dog would be good therapy for her father, who had been diagnosed with Alzheimer's disease. Because of his illness, he had to give up driving and could not go anyplace alone. His isolation and illness caused him to be depressed.

I, on the other hand, did not think having a dog would work. I was my husband's full-time caregiver and did not have time to care for a dog. I knew that if a dog was going to help him, it would need to be in the house. But having grown up on a farm, I was raised to believe dogs belonged outside.

Since my daughter volunteered at the local animal shelter, I should not have been surprised when she arrived at our home shortly thereafter with a scrawny, sickly female puppy about eight weeks old. The puppy was a mixed terrier and beagle weighing less than four pounds. My first instinct was to say, "No, it cannot stay here." Then I saw the joy on my husband's face as he cuddled the puppy in his arms.

"Let her stay for a couple weeks," my daughter insisted. "Then if it's not working for you, I will take her back."

I was still skeptical, but it sounded fair enough. Since we had to call the puppy something, we named her Skippy and moved her into a corner of the kitchen. She made herself right at home, and in no time she was sharing my husband's favorite chair, watching television with him.

Still, my intention was to ease Skippy out of my house after a few weeks. I knew I was in trouble, however, when we had to take her to the veterinarian for an overnight stay to be treated for a viral infection she had contracted while still at the pound.

While she was gone, my husband would ask over and over, "Where is Skippy?" or "When is Skippy coming home?" After that I did not have the heart to get rid of the puppy and disappoint my husband—which, of course, was my daughter's plan all along.

It was truly amazing to see how quickly my husband and his new friend bonded. The early morning walks were eagerly anticipated by both. Skippy slept in the kitchen, and she would wait for her master by the door each morning to go walking and to get the paper at the end of the driveway. Then, settling into their favorite chair, they would read the paper, watch TV, and nap for a couple of hours, freeing me to do things around the house.

There were times I could have sworn the dog was able to read her master's mind. She seemed to know instinctively when to be playful and frisky and when it was time to be quiet and lay her head on his knee and relax with him. At those times, my husband's hand would be caressing her head and back.

Having Skippy in our home meant more work for me—feeding her, cleaning up, and other chores necessitated by her being a house dog. She was housebroken within two weeks, so that was helpful. But the hours she freed up for me, the caretaker, by being a constant companion to my husband more than made up for the additional work she caused. He was more content to be alone in a room, and he was getting more outside exercise while walking Skippy. Plus all this activity helped snap him out of the frequent bouts of depression caused by the disease.

The routine established with his canine companion added a dimension to my husband's confused existence that neither I nor our children could accomplish. And his love and concern for her welfare was a mental challenge that otherwise would have been missing in his life.

In the evenings, as the sun set over the hill in back of our house, I would look out the window and see the two of them walking in the backyard, and I would say a silent prayer of thanks for the miracle of the scruffy, mixed-breed pound puppy I had not wanted. She gave my husband something to occupy his otherwise lost hours and brought him much happiness.

I still do not especially like dogs. But then Skippy was not just a dog. She became a member of our family.

Tennessee and Me

Brooke Nolen

I lay in bed very still. Someone was watching me. My eyes were closed, but I smelled his hot breath. Ouch! I felt pressure on my right ankle, and then he barked. I glanced over at the alarm clock. It was 7:30 a.m. and past the time to take Tennessee out. Many days my seventy-pound boxer had to step on me to help get me up in the morning. I was barely making it into work on time.

It had been over three months since my marriage ended, I was over five hours from my childhood home and family, and I had lost count of the number of tissue boxes I'd gone through. My friends and colleagues noticed that my laughter had stopped. Suddenly, my home life was very different. I felt alone.

Many days I wanted to just sleep, but I had others besides myself on a schedule in my condo. Even though I had recently given my rabbit to my best friend, I still had my fantail goldfish, a gray tabby cat, and Tenny—short for Tennessee, my

160

beautiful, white-chested boxer. Tenny sported white slippered paws and a homely pair of slightly crossed eyes. This adorable dog's morning step routine was my backup alarm clock for getting to work on time.

I had raised Tenny since he was eight weeks old. He had been the runt of the litter but had grown into a handsome specimen of his breed. He had these incredible facial expressions—he'd tilt his head ever so slightly to the side and purse his lips, as if to say "ahem" to try and get my attention. If I ate any kind of sandwich, he would give me his wide-eyed stare, and then drool would drip from his smiling mouth. He would patiently wait for a small piece of lunch meat or bread.

There was also, however, his attention-getting gas. The flatulence, which is characteristic of the breed, had notoriously interrupted prayer time with a group of friends. We all broke out in laughter. He may not have been reverent, but he certainly lived an innocent life. Seeing a squirrel while out for a walk or eating a nice piece of cheese were highlights of his day.

Even when he was several years old, Tenny was often mistaken for a puppy. Taking a stroll through a nearby park, he would try to greet everyone with a big lick or "kiss" on the face as he wiggled his rump with joy. Then there were the times when you just had to laugh as he walked straight into a light post or a parked car bumper.

161

One time he darted after a rabbit in a bush and plunged into a shallow pond. When he finally got himself upright, he just stood frozen in the shallow water. I waved casually to onlookers and quickly waded into the pond to get him. Ignoring their stares, I reached out my hand and grabbed the collar of my scared boy.

At home, I would catch Tenny and the tabby cat boxing each other. They would chase each other up and down the stairs—both instigating the games. This could go on for hours. They often needed a referee. The cat did lose a chunk of fur here and there, and Tenny nursed his nose on occasion. The "Nolen family zoo," as my friends called it, provided great entertainment for me in the evening. My pets never seemed to tire of this game. Eventually, however, Tenny and the cat would curl up next to each other and nap, usually on the couch with me as I watched TV or read a book.

I was keeping my life together in large part because of my pets and a few stubborn friends who insisted on checking on me. The cat and dog inevitably became most vocal when I was on the phone. Tenny would stick his face up to the cat sleeping on my lap and whine and sing—"waah waah waah"—which cut short more than a few talks. But Tenny was a great comfort. It was hard getting used to being alone, especially at night. He would often lick the tears from my cheeks after one of my crying binges at two in the morning. He knew when I was upset. He would bark if anyone came near the front door, including the geese from the pond, and I felt safe with him nearby.

My workdays became longer during our company's busy season. The cat just extended her naps, but Tenny grew more anxious. When returning from work, I would see Tenny peering down from my bedroom window as I approached the house.

One evening I opened the front door and saw a black Bible cover with embossed gold calligraphy in the entryway. The beautifully illustrated pages decorated the couch, littered the area rug, and poked out from my dining room chairs. This irreplaceable Bible was a going-away gift from my previous colleagues. My friends' signatures and encouraging messages were ripped to shreds. Slobber covered the book of Genesis. Was nothing sacred?

To err is human; to forgive, canine.

How could this have happened? The hefty Bible had been sandwiched between a novel and a large picture book on the middle shelf of the coffee table. Amazingly, the other two books remained in place on the shelf. It appeared the Bible had been pushed straight out of the stack to meet its own fate—and add more destruction to my life.

I didn't stop to think about the angry and destructive words that came out of my mouth next. I kicked the heap of torn pages in front of me.

Then I saw him in the corner of the room. Tenny dropped his head, sank back his shoulders, and folded his tail down as he peeked up with those homely eyes.

Suddenly I felt awful. Yes—awful that I had lost this special Bible, but more upset that I had recklessly yelled at one of my faithful companions. This wasn't the first time his behavior was less than perfect. He had literally colored my life with a box of crayons, spitting them out on the carpet after a good chew. And before that he ate my cell phone a month before

I was eligible for a new one. Losing this special keepsake on top of so many other losses brought my anger to a head.

I looked over at those big, droopy eyes and remembered how Tenny had licked my many tears. The vet had told me that Tenny may have faced his own separation anxiety during my long days at work. All he needed was a long walk and perhaps a good nap on the couch with me and the cat.

On the way to the park later that evening, I reflected on my crazy day while Tenny focused on a squirrel chattering in a nearby tree. My seventy-pound "puppy" suddenly tugged at his leash and pulled me back into the moment. Tenny had us at the base of the tree. He stood upright, jumping up and down on his hind legs to see the squirrel.

I felt the tension lessen in my shoulders as I smiled at the scene. Tenny barked excitedly and then looked back at me as if to say, "Aren't you coming?" We began to make our way back to the path. I realized that even with my messy life and relationships, I still had the simple joys of not-so-perfect pets—especially Tennessee, my faithful friend.

The Dog of My Heart

Pamela S. Thibodeaux

I'll never forget the Christmas Day my husband brought her home. At six weeks old, the puppy fit entirely in the palm of his hand. She was so tiny that I originally thought it was a rat! I wasn't too far off. Thib's Cajun Princess was a full-blooded rat terrier, the smallest female from the last litter out of his father's dog.

When I balked at having a dog in the house, my husband shrugged and said, "Oh well . . . we're gonna miss you." I still like to think he was teasing, but I didn't dare test him on the issue! Princess quickly became part of the family.

Fiercely loyal, Princess would abandon me on the couch in a split second if my husband asked, "Where's my puppy dog?" or simply said the word "traitor." He couldn't pump a hunting rifle or drag out the tackle box without her whimpering at the door, ready to go wherever he went. Although she and I grew to love each other immensely, there's no doubt that she was the dog of his heart.

Now let me tell you about the dog of *my* heart.

In 2004 we had to put Princess down at the advice of our veterinarian. For two years we talked often of getting another dog, but our hearts still hurt over the loss of our beloved pet. Then there were the issues of training a puppy and having to get someone to care for it when we travel—and, of course, dog hair in the house.

But each time we discussed the idea of getting another pet, I would tell my husband that I wanted a German shepherd. "Not a big, bulky cop dog, but a slick, slender female," I'd say, at a loss for better words to describe the beautiful canine I envisioned in my mind's eye.

The Bible teaches us to "Delight yourself in the LORD and he will give you the desires of your heart" (Ps. 37:4 NIV), and as Christians we're taught to listen to the still, small voice of God for wisdom, direction, and guidance. One June morning two-and-a-half years after losing Princess and debating whether or not we should get another dog, I headed out for my usual walk. When I heard that still, small voice urging me to go to the high school track, I obeyed. When I arrived, I noticed a dog running loose, a broken cable tied around her neck. The exact dog I'd described on numerous occasions to my husband—a German shepherd. *Slick. Slender. Female.*

I took the dog home and gave her some water. That afternoon my husband informed me that he'd discovered who her owners were. Reluctantly, we loaded her up in the truck and drove the few blocks to take her back. The moment I knocked on the door and asked if their dog was missing, the woman inside exploded. "That's it! That's the fourth time she's broken her cable. I'm getting rid of her." I learned the dog's name was Cassie. Then her owner asked me if I knew anyone who would give Cassie a good home.

We brought her home with us, and she's been mine ever since. The best news of all was that she was already house-broken and had been around children, which was an added bonus and a great relief since we had two young grandchildren and several great-nieces and great-nephews who visit often. Of course, we did have to deal with dog hair in the house and having someone care for her when we traveled. But those were minor hiccups compared to the joy of having her in our life.

There are stories of miracle pets—pets that save people or warn their owners of illness or impending danger. Cassie is our miracle pet.

Diagnosed with diabetes, my husband also suffered congestive heart failure and became disabled. Although she was clearly my dog, Cassie developed a special bond as a result of his being home with her all day.

A National Hero

Japan's most famous dog, Hachi-Ko, met his guardian every day at the train station, waiting as long as necessary for the man to come home. One day the man died while away at work. For nine more years Hachi-Ko continued to show up at the train station every day at the same time, waiting for his master. Today a statue exists in that train station in the dog's honor.[8]

For an animal that was left tied to a fence while Hurricane Rita raged through our area in 2005, she was extremely gentle and never aggressive in any manner, though she was terrified of storms. In addition to that, it was a rare thing to hear her bark. So early one morning when she went to our bedroom door and issued one short, sharp yap, hubby and I were both surprised. My husband, who'd been asleep at the time, got out of bed to see what the problem was. Then he sat at the table. Within moments of sitting down, he began to feel light-headed. His vision started fading. He rubbed his fingers together as a signal for me to check his blood sugar.

I immediately went into action and checked his blood sugar—which was dropping rapidly. Then I gave him something to drink and eat in order to bring his glucose level back up. All was well again.

This occurred on more than one occasion, where my husband's blood sugar would dip too low and Cassie would make noise. Somehow Cassie knew something was wrong with him, and her bark was intended to get him out of bed before his blood sugar dropped so low that he drifted from sleep into a diabetic coma. Nobody taught her this. She simply knew.

My husband passed away August 18, 2009. Though it is painful, I'm not traversing the journey through grief alone. I have the Lord Jesus by my side—and also the dog of my heart.

Sam and Tiffany

Sally Tolentino

I stared in disbelief, my jaw dropping to my chest. Huddled inside a filthy cage made of rusted chicken wire were at least fifteen whimpering little black standard poodle puppies. I had answered an ad in the paper and it had led me to this backwoods farm in South Carolina, but I had no idea that I would encounter such atrocious conditions.

My heart wanted to rescue every dog there. Knowing that was not feasible, I carefully chose the tiniest, dirtiest, most frightened pup in the cage. I noticed that her little paws were cut and raw from standing on chicken wire, and her coat was matted. She looked at me with sad yet hopeful eyes as I reached out for her and took her from the other pups, holding her trembling body in one hand. She was so very little for being eight weeks old, but the seller assured me it was safe to take her.

Since these dogs didn't have papers, I paid a minimal amount and left, cuddling my new puppy to my chest in an attempt to comfort her. I was happy to have rescued her, but saddened and angered at the thought of the puppies that remained behind.

Tiffany may have started life poorly, but the horror of those early weeks was soon forgotten as she became the queen of our house and hearts. Despite my vet's concerns that she would never develop to full size, she became the most elegant standard poodle you can imagine. Now I was sorry she didn't have papers, because her conformation and intelligence would have merited her being in the show ring. She looked stunning after a grooming with bright pink ribbons adorning her jet black ears, and she would prance around as if she knew she was gorgeous.

But the standard poodle was bred to hunt. Tiffany loved outdoor life on our six-acre horse farm more than she would have loved a beauty pageant. Hunting rabbits was her favorite pastime, but she was just as content to lazily lie on the back

The Hair of the Dog

Are you of the opinion that less hair on a dog equals less of an allergy problem? Not so! Of course, it's wise to remember that no dog is completely nonallergenic, but it turns out that *small, long-haired* dogs are best for people who have allergies.

First of all, a smaller dog means less fur altogether, which cuts down the problem right away. But longer fur actually means fewer allergens for sufferers. Why? Because short-haired dogs shed more often as their old hair is replaced with new hair. And that shedding means more and more dander—and more sneezing for some unlucky humans.

There of course are many breeds that work better than others for living with allergy sufferers, and you can find lists of those breeds on the Internet. Of course, cleaning a lot helps too—both the house and the dog.[9]

deck of our house and watch the horses graze in the pasture. She knew her boundaries, and my husband, Pedro, and I could fully trust Tiffany to never leave the farm . . . that is, until Sam came into her life.

Sam was our neighbor's German shepherd—a beautiful dog, beyond a doubt. But he became an awful nuisance as he began jumping over the fence and luring Tiffany to follow him on his daily adventures through the woods. It was apparent in no time that they had become best friends, and she would rather listen to his beck and call to roam the neighborhood than to our insistence that she stay put.

To our dismay, we had to take away some of Tiffany's freedom by making a fenced dog run for her so that she could not follow Sam. We thought we had the problem solved until we came home from work one day and discovered that Tiffany was gone. The pen was empty. We called her name in desperation, expecting her to bound out of the backwoods of our property with her usual joy (and maybe a little guilt after escaping from the pen). But she did not come. I frantically called my neighbor, Sam's owner, and was informed that Sam was safely at home. That's when I began to panic. If Sam was home, where was Tiffany? She would never leave without him.

Pedro and I searched by foot and by car, calling her name, but there was no response. A neighbor a few roads down said he had seen Sam and Tiffany earlier on the other side of the highway. So we looked much farther than we ever imagined she could have roamed, but to no avail. My heart pounded within my chest at the realization that we might never find her. As friendly, loving, and beautiful a dog as Tiffany was, maybe someone just picked her up and took her home. I imagined her leaping into a stranger's car and the person ridding her of her identification tag.

That thought was bad enough. More frightening still was the idea that I might find her lying hurt or even dead on the side of a road somewhere. I was frantic, but it got too late to look any longer, so we headed home. I never slept that night, and the next day I put posters up all over town offering a reward to anyone who had seen her. But the phone remained silent.

Pedro already had an attitude toward Sam that now had escalated to anger. He blamed him for Tiffany's disappearance. Not that Sam had a liking for my husband either, because he always met him with a low growl, as if warning him to keep his distance.

But late one afternoon, three days after Tiffany disappeared, the strangest thing happened. Sam came over to our yard and started barking at my husband, who was working in the garden. At first Pedro ignored the dog. "Go home, Sam!" Pedro commanded with audible irritation in his voice. Sam

started to run off but then turned back around and barked at Pedro, refusing to budge.

"I told you to go home, Sam. Now get!" Pedro scolded. Once again Sam started to run off, then abruptly turned and barked, refusing to go any farther.

It was then that a remarkable communication occurred between man and dog. Pedro suddenly realized that Sam was trying to get him to follow him. He approached the huge dog. Instead of being met with a growl, Sam looked at Pedro with approval and scampered toward the woods, all the while looking back to make sure Pedro was following him. Through the trees and brambles, dead leaves and branches, Sam led my husband into the woods and across a stream. Finally, Sam stopped and stood hovering over something.

As Pedro drew nearer, he could not believe his eyes. There was our Tiffany lying on the ground, seemingly lifeless, her thick coat caught in a terrible trap of brambles and thorns. Sam stood over her as if guarding her while Pedro worked frantically to free our precious dog. Dehydrated and weakened, but with no major injuries after being trapped for three days in the woods, Tiffany rose slowly to her feet, then happily kissed my husband's face. Sam stood nearby wagging his tail, as if aware of his great accomplishment. Our beloved dog was alive, thanks to Sam.

Sam and Tiffany remained friends for years. Fiercely devoted to one another, Sam would often visit Tiffany in her tightly secured run area. We now welcomed his appearance. This handsome brown-and-black German shepherd who once was an annoyance in our minds would forever be a hero in our hearts.

Taking Care of Ginger Blue the Beagle

Barbara Warner

The first time my husband and I saw the dog we now know as Ginger Blue the Beagle, she was in a twelve-by-six-foot cage just off our walking trail. She was dirty. And she was crying. The only way she could get out of the rain was to creep under a piece of metal that had holes in the top. I went over to pet her, but my husband didn't want to come with me. He was afraid he would come to love her. And then what would we do?

After that, I started visiting this little dog on a regular basis. Sometimes, when it was raining, I went at night to comfort her. She had dug some holes in the dirt to lie in, but they got muddy in the rain. The rain coming in through the holes in her metal house just made more mud.

I couldn't stop thinking about her. She was so skinny. And she had ear mites. She was never let out of her cage, and it was quite a mess. So I asked animal control to take a look at where she lived. I was sure the city would ask her owner to make some changes. But animal control said she had food, water, and shelter. That wasn't good enough for me.

One day, about two weeks later, I bought a doghouse and put a clean blanket inside it. Then I took it to the man who owned the dog he called Penny. He and his wife were watching a game show on TV when I came in, and it was very hard to talk over it. I told him we had made friends with his dog on our walks and that we had a doghouse we weren't using. We would be happy to give it to him. Would he accept it? After pondering the strangeness of this offer for some time, he finally agreed.

Penny's owner wasn't a mean man. He said his son had found the dog, and he was taking care of her. He didn't know where she came from. He had named her Penny, but I knew right off that name didn't suit her. One thing bothered me a lot after that visit. The man had said he wanted to breed Penny. I couldn't bear to see a bunch of puppies living in that dirty cage as well.

Penny's owner left the doghouse sitting outside her cage for many days. My husband and I continued to walk by the area, and I felt increasingly miserable. I continued to visit the dog and pet her through her cage. Her soft whining broke my heart.

One day the owner put the doghouse in Penny's cage. I counted it a small success, but the feeling didn't last. The rain and mud continued to pour into the doghouse, and the once-clean blanket got dirty and wet. I felt like Penny's circumstances hadn't improved much with my intervention.

Every time it rained I thought of her, and finally I couldn't stand it anymore. One day I got my checkbook and some cash. I bought a dog leash. I made an appointment with the dog groomer. Then, unbeknownst to my husband, I headed back to see Penny's owner. He was eating lunch when I sat down to talk to him in his smoky kitchen.

I told him how much I had grown to love his dog. I asked him if he would sell her to me. And then I waited. The man took a long time to think while he ate his meal. Finally he said, "I don't think I could sell 'er . . ." (My heart sank.) "I don't think I could sell 'er . . . for anything less than the $45 that I've put into 'er." It took me a moment to recover, but recover I did. I had been prepared to pay almost any price.

After I paid him, the man helped me get Penny out of her cage and into my car. "She's not leash trained," he said. I could see that immediately by the way she ran in all directions now that she was free. She was like a wild animal, sniffing everything. And as I would later learn, when a beagle's incredible sense of smell engages, everything else turns off, including their willingness to do anything you want them to do.

Finally, I got Penny into my car. She looked scared. I immediately drove her to the dog groomer, a bustling place filled with a cacophony of dogs barking and the smell of wet fur. This was a whole new world to Penny, and she started to shake. I did the best I could to comfort her, then handed her over to the technician with strict instructions to give her a good bath, cut her nails, and get rid of her fleas. I returned a few hours later to find a transformed dog. The dried mud was gone. In its place was a pretty little black-and-rust-colored dog with a white-tipped tail, white paws, and a little white dot on her left side. She sat there uncertainly, a small yellow bandana around her neck.

I then marched her to the veterinarian, where I needed no appointment. He gave me ointment for her ears and gave her a series of vaccinations. He said she was in pretty good health. And judging by her teeth, he thought she was about two years old. The vet talked to her kindly, but Penny was shaking again and wanted only to leave. She was eighteen pounds of determined muscle working her way to the door while I paid the first of what would be many veterinary bills.

I brought her home, but once inside she made a mess on the living room carpet. Given the poor quality of food she had been eating, her deposits were like rocks. I wondered what I had gotten myself into. How often would this happen? I showed her to a sage-colored, oval-shaped dog bed that I had bought for her and placed in a corner of the living room. There she staked her claim, curled up, and went to sleep.

By the time my husband came home, I had moved Penny and her bed to the bedroom. My husband said later that he had suspected something was up. The house just had a different feel to it. Sure enough, as I began to prepare him for our life-changing addition, a little dog with very big ears peeked tentatively around the corner at us.

My husband wasn't sure we could keep Penny, but he called the apartment owner and we got the green light. After all, we had been good tenants. They even changed the rental agreement to include "one little dog."

"What shall we call her?" I asked my husband. He thought for a moment. We remembered a dog named Ginger in a cartoon, but we thought that name wasn't very original. "She is partly ginger colored, though," I said.

"Remember that little resort town in Missouri that we drive through on the way to Kansas City?" my husband asked. "Wasn't it called Ginger Blue?"

It was perfect. And from then on "Penny" was officially Ginger Blue the Beagle.

That first night I had to leave to teach a class at the college, so I left Ginger Blue with my husband, not sure what would happen. When I came home three hours later, I found her on my husband's lap.

"Could you please take this dog off me?" he asked. "She's been sleeping here the whole three hours." She had just climbed up and made herself at home, seeking the security she had not had and cleverly cementing her relationship with my husband.

After that, Ginger Blue the Beagle became my husband's dog. And the chair my husband had been holding her in became her chair. Five years later, we still can't part with it, dilapidated wreck that it is.

One day, while my husband petted Ginger Blue's long silky ears (now free of mites) and the rain poured outside, it occurred to me: *You know, you can't take care of every problem. But in this world, it's a good thing to take good care of one little dog.*

Ginger Blue might have agreed, but she was asleep on our bed, warm and dry.

Bachernalia

Linda B. Greer

Pets were just an optional burden for me as a widow and the mother of two strong-willed daughters. My husband had tragically died when the girls were very young, and I had the staggering role of being both mother and father for many years. Other considerations against pets were the allergies my younger daughter and I both suffered due to cat dander and, to some degree, dog dander as well.

When my older daughter, April, grew up and got her own apartment in North Carolina, the first thing she brought to her home was a dog. Within a couple of years she had acquired two miniature schnauzer-mix puppies. April and her pups came to visit me in Florida, and I was hooked. Massive puppy withdrawal set in after April went back to North Carolina, and I craved a schnauzer!

Searching the newspaper in Orlando, I located a breeder in Lakeland. For my September birthday, my younger daughter, Dixie, and I drove down to procure not one but two male puppies from the same litter. Dixie helped name them. They became Bach and Mozart. We surmised that since schnauzers were a German breed, it was only logical to give them German-sounding names.

The first professional haircut the two received made an astonishing overhaul in their appearance. Before the transformation, Bach and Mozart had been little silver-and-white puff balls. Afterward they really looked like schnauzers. Boy, were they cute! On their first New Year's Eve, Dixie and I each had a little gray dancing partner as we ate snacks and welcomed the New Year.

I never realized how much paraphernalia is required to own dogs, since these were my first pets as an adult. There was the special puppy chow, the dog dishes for food and water, the dog crates, the endless rugs that had to be washed from wet puppy paws at the back door, the shots and trips to the vet, the collars, the leads, and the bath soap. Last but not least, a fence was eventually needed to keep them home.

Bach and Mozart were hardwired to roam every chance they got. Unfortunately, after about a dozen adventures, Mozart didn't return one day. Poor Bach's heart was so broken he had to be hand-fed for two weeks. We never did find Mozart.

After about two years, I moved from Florida to South Carolina. I took my Bach to a fenced yard that was three times bigger than the one he had in Florida. He loved it, but after a few months I could tell he was lonely while I was away. So the next Bach paraphernalia—or rather, Bachernalia—became a friend to play with: Sparks.

This time I wasn't taking the expensive route. Sparks was a rescued dog and cost very little to purchase. He turned out to be quite grateful and loyal for being rescued. He also wasted no time in letting Bach know he was no interloper but the number-one dog in the backyard. Sparks was basset hound from his neck to his tail, and had a terrier's head and stubbornness. Bach did not object at all to being second on the doggy totem pole. Thank goodness for an easy-to-please schnauzer.

After another year of being a two-dog family and an empty nest as far as children were concerned, my dogs became my children. The next step was teaching them manners. All went well until Christmas, when I had the brilliant idea to have a Santa picture of the three of us made at the local dog shelter.

Just out of curiosity, after our photo shoot I asked to see the dogs that were available for adoption. I had no intention

of adding to the Bachernalia collection. Oh, but there was a two-year-old, short-haired, chocolate-brown, bat-eared little whippet I just had to play with. He jumped up in my lap, licked my earlobe, and my resolve melted into mush. Batman was ours!

I rationalized Batman as a special Christmas present just for Bach and Sparks. Batman, though small, tried to win alpha dog status against Sparks, but he didn't take the throne away. He did, however, succeed in being the most afflicted dog I ever owned. The little critter was in the vet's office twice as much as Bach and Sparks combined within six months of his arrival.

Despite all the trouble, what's a mother to do when she just loves having little four-legged critters meet her with cheerful faces and wagging tails? Each time I come home I think, *This welcoming committee certainly tops a silent, dark house with no life.* These three amigos are now my "kids." I love them because they show me affectionate, unconditional love.

Even though all the Bachernalia has certainly put a hole in my pocketbook over these seven years, there's a moral to this story. You just can't have too much love or too many smiles to go around when you have dogs in your home. They make life interesting. You're always their best friend, every day.

Which often leads me to wonder: do I own them or do they own me?

Not a Boat, Not a Beaver—
It's a Lab!

Dee Aspin

*H*eel, Sammy and Benji," I repeated firmly.

Sammy, a male yellow Lab, thrust his husky chest forward, and Benji's schnauzer ears stiffened. Both were straining in the direction of my old friend Pam and her new friend—a healthy female yellow Lab. They walked the river trail three hundred yards ahead of us. The heritage trees sprouted branches high overhead, fanning each other in a graceful arc, creating a beautiful autumn archway. There was no doubt in my mind that God the Creator was watching out for at least two special females today, Pam and her new four-legged companion. The timing was too perfect.

Pam had phoned me just an hour ago. "I'm so glad you called me to meet."

"I couldn't sleep last night," I had complained, "and at 4:30 this morning I thought about giving you a call . . . we could meet at the river."

"I couldn't sleep last night either," Pam agreed, adding, "I tossed and turned." Lately she'd been through some arduous times.

We agreed to meet at 1:00 p.m. It had been a long time since we'd walked the river. Then I got another call from Pam that her morning plans changed. "Could you move the time up?" she asked. I wanted to beat the lunch rush traffic, so we agreed to meet at 11:30 at a section of the river where my dogs had never been.

We had walked and talked in a serious sort of way for such a bright and beautiful day. My friend was wading through some deep and dark waters that only God could carry her through, including two untimely deaths in a short time span.

"Dee, you better put Sam back on the leash!" Pam warned when I let him go for his water. The blue-gray river rushed by, and Sammy headed toward it. "Sam, come back—come now!"

We headed a mile up the river, and the water course changed as it tends to do. There was a wide, calm area where white egrets stood and ducks swam in the sunshine, enjoying the peace without a care in the world.

"Okay Sam!" I said, releasing his leash and inner tension. He whimpered and raced to the serene blue liquid, jumping in and paddling around like he hit heaven's shores.

"This is beautiful," Pam said, gazing across the broad river and up toward the island areas created by shifting ground and water levels. We stood still, silenced by beauty.

"Look! A beaver." I laughed, sighting a large head moving down the center of the river and leaving a wake behind it.

Pam and I admired the amazing ease of this creature in the water. As it drifted along undisturbed, the only thing breaking the smooth surface of the deeper waters, the head looked familiar but small. Then I realized it wasn't a beaver at all.

"It's a yellow Lab like Sam!" I exclaimed. We watched, waiting for her to turn toward shore. But she gazed straight ahead, never turning to the left or the right, swimming in an unwavering direction.

"Where is the owner?" I asked. I skimmed the edges on both sides of the river for human presence. Not a soul was in sight. "Two months ago Sammy got caught in the current," I told Pam as she too scanned the shorelines. I recalled those panicky moments when I threw the ball out too far on a dusky summer night and Sam, caught in the current and focused on the ball headed downstream, was oblivious to my calls. He would have continued down the center of the river if three fishermen downstream hadn't called him in together by yelling, "Sammy! Sammy!" and motioning him toward shore with all six of their arms.

Like Sammy, this Lab did not panic. She swam as though she were floating down the river on a cruise. She was focused. Her head and nose tilted above the water. She seemed comfortable, but where was she going?

"I don't think she knows what to do," I mused, "and she'll be hitting those rapids around the corner."

Pam cupped her hands to her mouth and waved. "Come here, girl!" she called in a higher than normal tone.

"Come over here!" I echoed, swinging my arms.

The Lab's head turned forty-five degrees in our direction. We both motioned. She glanced at us for only a moment and then stared straight ahead. We yelled louder and gestured more flamboyantly. Pam even jumped up and down. "Come on over here, girl!"

This time the dog turned her head and then her whole body. Sam and Benji were at the shoreline, and they both started barking. The Lab hesitated in the water. Now her face looked tense, and it was evident she was confused. She began to line herself up with the easy current. Pam doubled her efforts, and I chanted behind her.

The Lab now turned her body toward us and paddled to the encouragement on the sidelines. We were starting to breathe easier the closer she got. "She'll make it," I assured Pam. "Labs are water dogs, they can go the distance."

As the dog neared the shallow waters, I was so focused on her that I did not see Sam on the sidelines. He was in dominance mode. The Lab was on solid ground now, but she cowered. Sammy's back bristled and he suddenly jumped on her, gripping her haunches with his front paws.

"Doggonit, Sam!" I grabbed Sam's collar as he let loose and quickly leashed him and Benji. Yellow girl turned to head back out again.

"Use these to coax her." I tossed Pam some dog biscuits and left her two extra leashes I had brought as extensions. "I'm taking Sammy and Benji out of view. We'll be waiting down the path; she'll never come with them around now— she's frightened." I headed off, coaxing my excited dogs and so thankful to have those extra leashes today.

We waited awhile. I paced, hoping Pam was able to leash the yellow girl so she wouldn't run off. Through the tall grass, I caught sight of Pam's head in a stooped position. I realized she was bending over the dog; they must be connecting. Eventually Pam rounded the bend with a confident-looking

Saving the Snow Dogs of Japan

Only since the post–World War II years has the Akita—a handsome, intelligent, and loyal breed from Japan—been valued worldwide. One Japanese World War II veteran, Morie Sawataishi, lived in the remote mountainous region of his country, and at the age of thirty began raising and giving away Akitas, commonly called Snow Dogs. He had become distressed during the war to see this breed being slaughtered for their thick fur, which then was used to line officers' coats.

At the time Sawataishi started to raise his puppies, there were sixteen Akitas left in the country—and two of them were his own. The remarkable story of this man's lifelong mission to save the Akitas can be read in the book *Dog Man* by Martha Sherrill.[10]

female Lab, leashed and pulling her quickly along like she knew where she was going.

I looked at Pam's face. It was relaxed and had a special shine, the kind of shine that shows something good has happened inside of us. Sammy, Benji, and I walked a good hundred yards behind Pam and her dog, who were inhaling the fresh, cool air and enjoying the autumn wonderland. It was a glorious day. I peeked through the shrubs, now close to rougher rapids, and felt thankful we were all safe and back to our starting point.

Pam called the owners multiple times, but the message box answered full. Then she called the county, and finally a California ranger came by and took the female Lab.

After the exchange, Pam looked joyful. "It was such a short time but I feel like we really bonded," she said. "I'm going to miss her." Her mouth smiled but her eyebrows frowned.

Before we parted, we paused for a moment and prayed. Pam thanked God for the opportunity to rescue the dog—for all the things that fell into place for us to be at that place at that time. She prayed the ranger would easily contact the owners. "And God," her voice broke, "sometimes it seems the waters of life will overwhelm us, but you always come in, even at the last moment, and save us. You won't let us drown."

As I drove away, it seemed the autumn leaves swirling to the ground were dancing with joy. My friend was going to be all right.

The dog's owner, whose name was also Dee, and her son Sean, had been looking for their Lab five hours by the time she got our messages. The ranger took the dog to the shelter. The next morning Dee picked her up, happy and in good spirits. The Lab had floated down the river at least four miles from where they lived. And here's what's fun: not only do the owner and I have the same name, but her son's name, Sean, is the masculine form of Pam's daughter's name, Seana.

Pam said that day at the river was the best day she'd had in weeks. And it seemed to be one more connection in a good, mysterious circle in her life.

The Foo Foo Dog

Cathy E. Watkins

*L*exi is my little shih tzu and my very best friend. In my upbringing, Lexi would be called a "foo foo dog." To understand what she means to me, you need to know that a tomboy like me always laughed at people with foo foo dogs. I never realized how much love they can bring to your life.

I grew up in North Carolina during the fifties and sixties in a family of five kids. Daddy always had hunting dogs that were as good as any professionally trained dogs, but they were not to be considered pets. They had a role in helping him gather wild game for our dinner table. We weren't actually poor but we did need that extra food, and there was never money for each of us to have a pet.

But there was always another dog around the house, and that was the family pet. These were mostly what people called "sooners"—dogs that would just as soon be one breed as another. That dog's favorite human was whoever slipped it treats from the table or let it sleep at the foot of the bed.

That person was usually me. Rules of the house said no dogs sleeping in the bed, but I was the bravest of the kids when it came to breaking that rule.

Throughout those childhood years, we had a mixed cocker spaniel, German shepherds, small terriers, and basset hounds. We also had what people called "feist" dogs, as in the meanest dog in town—or at least the dog thought it was. Some of these dogs found us after they had been abandoned, and some were given to us by friends or family. Their names were Rex, Tinkerbell, Big Stick, Fancy Pants, Max, and Princess. I'm not sure where all the names came from, but they usually had a lot to do with the dog's personality.

Tinkerbell was a little feist who loved the attention from all us kids but slept in my bed most of the time. Big Stick was a solid black feist and only about seven inches tall. He would attack anything that he thought was trespassing on his domain, and he even survived fifty stitches to his belly after fighting with a Doberman. He got his name because Daddy said he was a little dog that carried a big stick.

My female basset hound, who I took with me when I moved out, was named Fancy Pants because she looked like she had brown pants on her rear. We tried to breed Fancy since she was registered, but she didn't really like the full breed bassets. She preferred a Lab who lived next door. Being the escape artist that she was, she visited him during her special time and the result was five puppies ranging in looks from bassets to Labs to a mix of both.

We gave all the puppies away except for one, and his name was Maximillion, Max for short. His head and tail were Lab and his body was all basset. As you can imagine, he was very funny looking and people always asked what kind of dog he was. We always believed Max was mentally challenged because he never left Fancy Pants's side. She cleaned him like a puppy until the day she died.

Fancy and Max were alive when my husband, Mike, and I moved away from my hometown of Kannapolis, North Carolina, and the dogs went with us. That was the first time I lived outside my hometown, so those dogs' companionship was important as I adjusted to being away. Being from a big family and always living within a mile of the home I was raised in made adjusting to living thirty miles away difficult for me.

But losing my dogs later on was harder. After losing Fancy Pants and eventually Max, I decided I did not want another dog. I get attached to animals quickly and consider them to be my best friends. I just didn't want to lose another pet.

The years passed and we had strays come around from time to time, but usually they found their home or just never stayed. And there were cats.

Have you ever known an animal that acted practically human? Norman, our first house cat, was that way. He was a short-haired gray cat with gold-green eyes who was born to a pair of barn cats. Mike spotted him at once in the litter and thought he looked like a cat he could relate to. Mike named the cat Norman. From Norman's first day at home until his last day at home, he was Mike's buddy.

Norman helped us through a lot of hard times and never once said a bad word about anyone—except for the cat down the street, that is. When Mike and I started working on the NASCAR circuit and traveling, we were able to leave Norman with family. But when we came home from a two- to six-week trip, Norman would not leave Mike's side.

Eventually I decided to come off the road and Mike continued to travel. While I was home alone, Norman was my constant companion and gave me a lot of love. He slept on Mike's side of the bed when Mike was gone and always between us when Mike was home. Norman was with us for fifteen years.

I have never grieved or felt such pain at losing a pet like I did with Norman. When my daughter Shelly told me she had another pet to take his place, I bucked at that because no other pet could ever take Norman's place.

Shelly's boyfriend had a year-and-a-half-old shih tzu named Lexi, and when they visited me they always brought the dog along. Even though shih tzus are foo foo dogs, I had been very protective of Norman and would not let them bring the dog in the house while the cat was alive. Lexi was just a little thing who wanted to play, but Norman did not have the patience for her. I resisted the urge to even pet Lexi.

Of course, after Norman's death Lexi came to visit more often. During a visit one day, I was asked to keep Lexi for a couple weeks while her human was working out of town. I was so heartbroken about losing Norman that I thought nothing could ever take his place in my heart. Boy, was I wrong. That little dog latched onto my heartstrings and started healing my broken heart. It amazed me how much energy and excitement such a little dog had. But she belonged to someone else, so I was afraid to get attached.

Lexi lived in a mobile home with a smoker and got very little sunlight or fresh air. Since she had some skin problems, I took on the task of helping her get her skin sores cleared up. After I took her to the vet for a thorough checkup, I started feeling responsible for her health and well-being. When she had been at my house for a while, she blossomed. Her hair had a healthy shine again. Her owner asked me if I would like to keep her forever. What a thrill!

This little baby of a dog has taken on the responsibility of family pack leader for our household. When she walks, she constantly looks back to make sure I am following just like a good pack follower should. She stays by my side as if she knows I need her love and protection. She does not bark unless teased or encouraged to "talk." She makes a little whimper of a noise when she wants to go out. She sleeps with me, gets treats on a regular basis, and is my favorite "person" in the world. We play the game of hiding treats in places around the house. I can say, "Go find a treat," and she runs as fast as she can, spinning on the slippery kitchen tile.

My life and daily schedule revolve around Lexi, and that is just fine with my husband. She has latched onto his heart-strings too. She makes us laugh more than ever.

Who would have believed that a foo foo dog could repair my broken tomboy heart? But Lexi did it.

Love Once More

Sherri Gallagher

My stomach knotted and ached. I could barely drag myself out of bed, and I had to change the tear-soaked pillow daily. I wanted to hide in sleep and pretend she was there beside me, her black muzzle resting on my shoulder and her deep breaths a rhythmic lullaby. In the space of an instant, my search and rescue partner, my beautiful German shepherd, was gone, hit by a motorcycle.

Tears dripped onto my keyboard as I read this email: "You have our deepest sympathy over the loss of your dog. However, you must realize this puts the team in a difficult situation. We were counting on Clara for the national Top Off drill in a few weeks. Please let us know how you are going to resolve this problem. We will work at this end to fill the roster."

Didn't they understand? I'd lost more than just a dog! Clara wasn't a tool or commodity to be replaced with a quick phone call. Clara had understood me as no dog ever had. She cuddled when I needed it or hit a scent at a thousand yards and barreled away to find the person who had her toy, sure of my location and response to her actions. I had lost my best friend and these people were worried about a stupid training exercise.

I wiped my face with the back of my hand and called Clara's breeder, Julie.

"Hey you, how you holding up?" Julie's cheerful sympathy set off another round of tears.

"Not so well. If I want to stay on the state team, I have to come up with a dog—immediately. An adult, mostly trained." Tears choked my voice.

"What did you have in mind? Do you want to look at the adults I have here? I don't think any of them are really what you want, but you're welcome to look and test them and take anything you think will work." Trust Julie and her generous heart. Those German shepherds were her livelihood and yet she had just given me carte blanche to take what I needed.

"Actually, I need your opinion and maybe a phone number." I grabbed a tissue. "At the International Kennel Club dog show, a couple approached us about a male German shepherd they wanted to sell to a working home. Ula was the mother and Zillo was the father, so with that bloodline he must be a pretty intense working dog. And he had to come from your kennel."

"What's his name?"

"Lektor. What do you know about him?"

There was a slight pause. It sounded like Julie sniffled too. "You would be perfect for each other. I think it would be the saving of you both."

"What's wrong with him?"

"Nothing. That's the problem. He's a very high-drive, working-line male with nothing to do. They wanted the best training for a working dog, so they sent him to Germany to train in tracking, obedience, and protection. He earned his Schutzhund I title and a bunch of others before he was shipped home. The Germans were so impressed they didn't want to send him back. His current owners don't have time to work him. He's two and a half, six months younger than Clara, and still able to bond to a human."

"Yeah, but is this human able to bond to a new dog right now?"

Julie didn't attempt to answer that one.

Four days later Lektor arrived at my door. The entire search team, past and present members, were enclosing my side yard with a six-foot chain-link fence. The place resembled O'Hare Airport with all the people coming and going, motors running, and heavy tools getting tossed from person to person. Anyone not digging postholes or stringing fence crowded into my tiny kitchen, cooking for the team members working outside.

A handsome couple got out of a pickup truck and the husband reached into the dog crate in the back. A huge black sable shepherd exploded out of the truck, instantly hitting the end of an eight-foot leash. The man demonstrated the dog's obedience. The dog reminded me of a caged lion, waiting to unleash mayhem.

I turned to my husband, more than a little intimidated by the dog. "Do you think I can handle him?"

He smiled and hugged me. "You're probably the only person on the team who can. Write them a check."

I still had my reservations. I invited them inside and watched the reaction of Lektor to my other dogs. First came blind Taz.

At ten, an inoperable brain tumor had stolen her sight and gradually her fat reserves. But she still ran the place as alpha dog, and this would be the biggest test Lektor would face. If there was a problem, he would not be staying.

Lektor had a good thirty pounds on Taz and moved like lightning to her arthritic molasses. She cornered him coming through the door, pinned him to the wall, sniffed him all over, and nudged him around like a mother would her puppy. Lektor dropped his head lower than hers and moved wherever she wanted him. Fully capable of slicing her to pieces, he gently acknowledged her as queen.

Next came our four-year-old Afghan hound, Crunch. Since we just lost Clara, Crunch had nibbled at his food and lay on the sofa with his head hanging over the arm. The two dogs had been playmates and he clearly missed her. Lektor and Crunch sniffed noses and ignored each other.

Lektor lay down in the dining room while people hurried back and forth, stepping over his prone form. One of the handlers had brought her five-year-old daughter. Every inch of her little body indicated boredom. She motored over to Lektor and pulled his ear before I could intervene. He ignored her.

I turned to his owners. "How is he with children?"

They both smiled. They'd seen the interaction between the girl and Lektor and had confidently ignored it. "He's great with kids. Our daughter used him as her 4-H project. No problem."

Their confidence relaxed my concerns, and I watched the interaction between dog and child without interfering. The girl found the dog toy basket and tossed the dog an old tug. He snatched it out of the air without rising from the down position and snapped his powerful jaws shut. She laughed and hurried over to him. Grabbing the tug handle, she pulled. Lektor held on. That brought giggles and a smile. Grabbing with both hands, she leaned her entire weight into pulling on the tug. Lektor held on and didn't move, holding her with just his powerful neck muscles.

Shifting position, the child stuck one hand in the gap the tug created between his teeth. Lektor immediately opened up, working his tongue to get the human appendage out of his mouth. She took away the toy. He waited, watching the tug intently but holding his down position. The little girl smiled, tossed it back, and played tug, using the method of her hand shoved into the dog's mouth to get him to release the toy. His gentleness with the little girl relieved my misgivings. After all, in search and rescue we're supposed to bring them back alive, not slightly gnawed.

I took a deep breath. Time to find out what this living keg of gunpowder would cost. They showed me the receipts for his training in Germany—over $10,000 worth, and that did not include his purchase price. They had an offer from a celebrity looking for a guard dog to patrol his estate, but Lektor would be a kennel dog without serious human contact and they wanted a home life for him. They liked seeing my dogs comfortably enthroned on the couch. They wanted that for Lektor. They also knew he needed to work, and I would be using him for search and rescue. They had discussed it, and he was mine for $4,000. I wrote the check. They hugged Lektor and left.

I always trained my dogs at sunrise. Lektor obviously had been worked in the evenings. That first morning he yawned, stretched, and looked at me like he had a hangover. I grabbed a tug and he did the Dr. Jekyll to Mr. Hyde switch. Eyes alert and focused intently, he tried to steal the toy from my hand, bouncing his hundred-plus pounds off my hip repeatedly. I struggled to keep my balance and hold on to the toy.

First things first: would he obey me? A deer took off from my orchard, and Lektor launched straight for the road, hot on its heels. Visions of Clara's body and sightless eyes slammed into my mind. I screamed Lektor's name over and over. He ignored me and disappeared out of sight through the trees.

I collapsed in a ball on the ground, sobbing. I waited to hear the screech of tires and deadly thump that would herald his death. Silence, then heavy breathing, and a large tongue slurped my neck. I sat up hugging his mud-slimed, burr-coated body. He went to work cleaning my face with a tongue that could lick the cheese from a large pizza in two swipes. Obviously, we needed to work on control.

Lektor's obedience training must have been done with force. I found a ridge of scar tissue on his neck telling me just how much force had been used. If I did a recall and told him to down before he got to me, he would lay back his ears, duck his head, and crawl to reach me, every muscle tensed in anticipation of the pain from a correction. We needed to start over.

Using boiled beef liver, we worked on the obedience. Speaking softly to force him to concentrate, I switched commands to English when the German word he'd been trained with brought out a stress reaction. Within a few days, the jingle of the obedience collar brought him dancing and excited to my side, ready for playtime.

I still missed Clara horribly, and on more than one morning I rolled over, crying uncontrollably. I didn't want to care about Lektor. Losing Clara was a raw, bleeding wound, and there wasn't room for a dog. But having learned training came in the morning, Lektor came to get me as soon as the sky started to lighten. He would jump up, landing with his bony elbows digging into my chest while dropping his slobber-covered ball on my face. He took away the option of staying in bed and dragged me back from the abyss. It was get up or have tears licked away.

One morning before dawn, Lektor came to get me. No ball. No friendly jump up. Instead I got a loud whine and strong, almost painful shoves with his nose. I'd spent enough time with shepherds to know trouble hovered nearby.

I jumped out of bed. "What is it?"

Lektor hurried away, looking over his shoulder and moving forward as soon as I started to follow. He took me straight to Taz, who was in the throes of a grand mal seizure. I stroked her until the seizure stopped but another followed almost immediately.

I yanked jeans and a sweatshirt on over my nightgown, kicked into loafers, and grabbed my purse. At a break between seizures, I coaxed Taz into my SUV and rushed to the emergency vet. The tumor had grown more, and it was time to say good-bye. I held her in my arms as they gave her the shot, and she slipped away. In the space of five weeks I'd lost both my canine partners. They had been almost as close to me as children and certainly had been my best friends. It was all up to Lektor now. Like it or not, it was time for me to accept and love him.

I had signed up to take Clara to a disaster search training seminar in Connecticut along with two other team members. I called and they switched Lektor in for Clara.

Lektor sat quietly in hectic O'Hare Airport. He ignored everyone and everything in the crowded hallways. People had one of two reactions—a gushing "Can I pet your dog?" or a face-blanching, hug-the-wall move to get around him.

We started down the Jetway and Lektor's relaxed stroll morphed into a muscle-tensed, crouching stalk. He leaned hard against my leg and glanced around with swift movements. The smell of aviation fuel must have triggered memories of his flights to and from Germany. On board, I murmured soothing phrases and slipped into my seat. Lektor crawled into my lap and buried his head in my neck. My teammate across the aisle laughed uproariously and threatened to dig out his camera. All he could see were my legs and head sticking out around my huge dog. I coaxed Lektor onto the floor where he lay, panting heavily.

A man got on the plane and turned to the flight attendant. "I'm not sitting next to that dog."

"Not a problem, sir." The attendant picked up the microphone. "Would anyone like to switch seats and sit next to a search and rescue dog?" A sea of hands filled the air, and a teenage girl climbed in next to us. The third man in the row had a son working as a canine officer. He stretched out, tipped his seat back, and went to sleep. Lektor used the man's ankles as a pillow. By the time we reached LaGuardia, dog and man snored in unison.

The first night in the hotel room, Lektor stood guard at the door. Anyone passing along the walkway hurried their steps after he rumbled a deep-chested growl. The morning found us both exhausted from a restless night.

On an obstacle course, Lektor slipped, banging both his knees. At first he refused to put his weight on one leg, eventually standing on it but obviously uncomfortable. I was crying. After class, my teammates and I visited a couple of attendees who had a car full of first aid gear. They handed me an ice pack for Lektor along with some sage advice: "Get over it. SAR dogs get hurt and heal."

I applied ice to Lektor's knee while he relaxed on his side. A teammate explained the situation to the others and they left me alone. I sat on the sidewalk with my dog, letting conversation flow around me in unheard words. I'm not sure how much later Lektor and I staggered up to our room and collapsed on the bed. We fell asleep next to each other while I held an ice pack on his injuries and he snored in my ear.

From that day on, Lektor was mine and I was his. Wherever I sent him, he went without hesitation. I refused searches that put his life at risk. His obedience and tracking improved to the point where he earned his Schutzhund III title, and he once tracked a potential suicide victim across paved parking lots and roads in the pouring rain.

Lektor is my current partner along with Belle, a niece of Clara's. At nine he is still a showstopper and my go-to boy. I think we've had close to fifty search assignments, mostly deep wilderness, and he's always delivered everything he had to give. He recently fathered a new litter of puppies, and I'm taking a son of his named Kobalt to train. One thing is sure, this boy won't be the same as Taz or Clara or Lektor or Belle. But who would want that? I've learned there will always be room in my heart for one more four-footed friend.

Lektor came to me when sorrow was a lead weight sinking me into darkness, a pit I didn't want to climb out of. There was no fight left in me, a fighter since I was knit in my mother's womb. God sent a hundred-pound, four-footed angel to drag me back to the world of the living, to a world where I could make a difference. In doing so, he opened a path of joy and peace for both of us.

The House in the Woods

Anonymous

*I*n the Alcoholics Anonymous tradition, working the Twelve Steps helps many people get sober and stay sober. I'm one of them.

At age thirty-two, I stopped drinking alcohol and started dealing with my problems. With the help of a wise sponsor, I began working the Twelve Steps and had reached the fourth and fifth steps in the program. *Alcoholics Anonymous*, the guidebook commonly called "The Big Book," states those steps as:

> Step 4: Made a searching and fearless moral inventory of ourselves.
>
> Step 5: Admitted to God, to ourselves, and to another human being the exact nature of our wrongs.[11]

These steps felt daunting to me, but I wanted to do what I needed to do. I was encouraged by my sponsor to think of times in my life that caused me to feel guilt, shame, or anger. Then I was to list those episodes, commenting on each as honestly as I could.

I did exactly that, writing in longhand on a yellow, legal-sized tablet every wrong I'd committed as well as every negative feeling I had toward anyone who had ever treated me badly. This took several pages. My sponsor felt I would be better off telling his own sponsor what I had to say, and he sent me to her. She was an older woman who lived deep in the country north of the city where I lived, and she invited me to her home.

I drove down a lot of woodsy, curving roads through lake country to get to her house. I don't remember her name. I

doubt she's even alive today. What I remember most about my confession to this kind stranger were her two dogs. At the front door of an old, sprawling, comfortable house with lots of windows, this wonderful woman greeted me and introduced me to her two fat and friendly Welsh corgis.

My hostess was unusual. For one thing, even though I'm not a tall woman, she was much shorter than I am. In addition to that, she was stooped over in such a way that she could not face me directly. She could only bend at the waist, turn her head, and look up sideways in order to see my face. When she did, I saw that she had a kind smile and bright, lively eyes.

She invited me to have a seat on a flowered, very lived-on sofa that was under a huge picture window. The dogs waddled after me. The woman sat down across the room in an easy chair, but since her physical condition made it so taxing for

Turn Your Talents to the Dogs!

If you knit or crochet, think about using your handicrafts for your local shelter. Call the shelter personnel to see if they might like something comfy for their dog cages. They will most likely be delighted to accept knitted or crocheted items from you.

A cage blanket is uncomplicated to make, and a dog doesn't care how fine your work may or may not be—a dog just wants to be cozy. Use washable yarn, of course, and leftover scrap yarns are just fine. Be sure to call first and ask the facility what it can use and what dimensions your end result should be.

If you can't knit or crochet, consider donating to the shelter any blankets or afghans you don't want anymore. Vermonter Eric Robinson, a knitting volunteer who termed these cage blankets "snuggles," has this surprising and happy observation: "An animal is more likely to be adopted if it has a blanket in its cage."[12]

her to look at me, she simply looked at the floor and told me to go ahead when I was ready.

I pulled out my moral inventory list and started reading from it and expounding on what was written. This was a mighty long, difficult task. Since nobody was actually looking at me, it was a little easier to be forthright, but talking about the past was still rather wrenching for me. And since there was no eye contact to be made, I looked out the picture window as I talked. I discovered that the yard was filled with dozens of wild rabbits. As dusk approached, the rabbits frolicked, hopping in and out of the woods. It felt like I was in the middle of a fairy tale, and I found it comforting.

Even more comforting, however, was the presence of the two corgis. I recognized them as the favorite breed of England's royals, often photographed accompanying the Queen. Corgis are short, elongated, and oddly regal themselves with their big, handsome heads and intelligent faces. These corgis had moved away from their owner and joined me at the couch, where they parked their long, chunky bodies on either side of me. They both hunkered down and leaned into my legs. By nature they are herding dogs, and I felt nicely tucked in by them. It was as if they knew I needed bolstering. The two corgis reminded me of the Foo dog statues I used to see in New York's Chinatown—big lionesque creatures that flanked front doors. Statues of these mythical animals had guarded sacred sites in China in ancient times.

That day at the house in the woods, where the rabbits gathered and the dogs stayed nearby, I too began to feel I was part of something sacred. I felt God had specifically sent me to this place full of life to meet this kind, bright-eyed woman.

As she listened to me without judgment and as her calm, fat dogs pressed against me, I felt safe and valued.

When I finally stopped talking, my hostess spoke quietly. "My dear," she said, "the first person you need to forgive is yourself."

She was right, of course. I felt immediate relief. I can now say with complete confidence that some ugliness inside me died that day in her living room, and I've been much kinder to myself since then.

Years later I would think of that day as I sat with my mother during her dying weeks. Her two dogs—a golden Lab and a schnauzer—sat with her too, one on either side, for the time it took my mother to die. I was glad those handsome, loyal beasts joined us for that hard yet blessed time.

I completed the Twelve Steps, and I've been sober a long time now. I'm grateful to God for every morning I have. I'm grateful for the stooped, bright-eyed woman in the woods and the rabbits in her yard, and especially for her dogs. I still can feel those noble corgis pressed against me, as if to say, "It's all right. Take heart. We're here with you."

Acknowledgments

*M*any thanks to the talented and patient writers in this book who gave me the privilege of using their stories. Many more thanks to the wonderful people at Revell, a division of Baker Publishing Group, who worked hard to make this book a reality.

And a special thanks to my gracious editor, Vicki Crumpton.

Notes

1. "The Kitty Rx," *Good Housekeeping*, August 2008, 38.

2. Martha Sherrill, *Dog Man: An Uncommon Life on a Faraway Mountain* (New York: Penguin, 2008), 4.

3. From *Prevention,* October 2008, 5.

4. Grady Timmons, *Waikiki Beachboy* (Honolulu: Editions Limited, 1989), 35.

5. Temple Grandin and Catherine Johnson, *Animals in Translation* (New York: Scribner, 2005), 115.

6. Cesar Millan, "The Dog Whisperer: What Your Pet Can Teach You," *Parade*, January 11, 2009, 10–11.

7. "Catching Up with Marley's Master," *People*, January 12, 2009, 43; "Walter Scott's Personality Parade," *Parade*, February 1, 2009, 3.

8. Sherrill, *Dog Man*, 4.

9. Dr. Marty Becker and Gina Spadafori, "Have a Pet without Sneezing," *Parade*, February 8, 2009, 10–11.

10. Sherrill, *Dog Man*, 5–6.

11. *Alcoholics Anonymous*, 3rd ed. (New York: Alcoholics Anonymous World Services, 1976), 59.

12. Betty Christiansen, *Knitting for Peace: Making the World a Better Place One Stitch at a Time* (New York: Stewart, Tabori & Change, 2006), 64–65.

Contributors

Anonymous has been sober since 1985.

Dee Aspin is an inspirational writer and speaker and a native of the Golden State. She enjoys daily romps with her yellow Lab and mini schnauzer. A guest writer for cbn.com, she authored *Lord of the Ringless* (see www.Lordofthe Ringless.com) and has published poetry, articles, and animal and human interest stories for Barbour, *Guideposts*, and *Today's Christian Woman* among others. Visit Dee at www. DeeAspin.com.

Kelly Pickett Bishop is a mom of two boys and lives in eastern Pennsylvania. She is currently working on her first novel as well as some short stories for various web publications.

Catherine Ulrich Brakefield has been published in magazines, newspapers, and books, and she is the author of *The Wind of Destiny* and *Images of America—The Lapeer Area*. Her writings exemplify her love for people and animals. She and her husband, Edward, live in Addison Township, Michigan, where they raise Arabian horses, puppies, kittens, and chickens. See www.catherineulrichbrakefield.com for her newest releases.

Sandy Cathcart lives in the highlands of southern Oregon where she writes about the Creator and everything wild. She is currently at work on her nonfiction book *Wild Woman*, and recently finished her novel *Shaman's Fire*. She is the owner of www.needlerockpress.com, and she displays her art and writing at www.sandycathcart.com.

Over the last ten years, **Lorilee Craker**'s basset hound (well, her husband's hound), Dinah Blue, has grown on her. When she's not letting the dog out, shushing her, feeding her, or trying to interpret her doggie talk, Lorilee has written eleven books, including the *New York Times* bestseller *Through the Storm* with Lynne Spears and *Sharing, Saving, and Shoofly Pie: Money Secrets of the Amish*. A native of Winnipeg, Manitoba, Lorilee lives in Grand Rapids, Michigan, with her husband, Doyle; their three kids, Jonah, Ezra, and Phoebe; Dinah Blue; two cats; and a cockatiel.

Cindy Crosby is the author of five books, including *By Willoway Brook* and *The Ancient Christian Devotional: Cycle C*. She's contributed to several other books, including *Creation Care* and *A Life of Prayer*. Her writing has appeared in many publications, among them *Backpacker*, *Chicago Wilderness*, *Christianity Today*, *Books & Culture*, *Christian Century*, and *Publishers Weekly*. A former National Parks Artist in

Residence, Cindy enjoys backpacking, kayaking, and the wonders of God's amazing creation.

C.J. Darlington's first novel, *Thicker than Blood*, was the winner of the Christian Writers Guild's 2008 Operation First Novel contest. Her second novel, *Bound by Guilt*, has just been released. She is cofounder of the Christian entertainment website www.TitleTrakk.com. A homeschool graduate, she makes her home in Pennsylvania with her menagerie of dogs and a cat named Cubby. Find out more about her online at her website www.cjdarlington.com.

Andrea Doering is an editor, wife, mother of three, and happy walker of Honey, the family's lovable hound. Honey joined the Doering family about a year ago, and when she's bored, she goes after shoes left by the door. The result? Honey has succeeded where this author failed for years—the children now pick up their shoes every day.

Chrissy Drzewiecki has been writing poetry and stories since she was a little girl. She is currently writing a children's short story series and dabbling with writing Christian romance. Chrissy works as an administrative assistant, and she lives in Rancho Cordova, California, where she also enjoys reading and gardening. She and her husband have two wonderful grown boys and four grandchildren.

Gwen Ellis is the author of the *Read and Share Bible* storybook, several other Read and Share products, and many other books. She owns Seaside Creative Services, an editorial and writing business. She lives in Port Hueneme, California. Check her out at www.seasidecreativeservices.com.

Ann H. Gabhart got her first puppy at the age of nine, about the same time she decided to be a writer. Since then she's had at least one dog and usually two or more to keep her company down on her Kentucky farm while she keeps writing her stories. She has published more than twenty books, including the bestselling Shaker novels *The Outsider*, *The Believer*, and *The Seeker*, and her latest book of historical fiction, *Angel Sister*. Visit her website at www.annhgabhart.com.

Sherri Gallagher has lived with German shepherds almost all her life, except when she took a small foray into Afghan hounds. She continues to train dogs and handlers for canine search and rescue and also goes out on searches with her own dogs. She cross-trains her dogs for the sport of Schutzhund. You can learn more about her and her canine partners at www.mybodyguarddogs.com or the search team at www. gssarda-il.org.

Callie Smith Grant loves animals of all kinds. She is the author of many animal stories, the author of several books for young readers, and the compiler of the anthologies *A Prince among Dogs* and *A Dickens of a Cat*.

Linda B. Greer is a Christian author and freelance writer from the upstate of South Carolina. She also works part-time as a professional academic tutor and standardized test coach. Her publications include a devotional writer's blog *Spiritual Heartbeats* (spiritualheartbeats.blogspot.com).

Alison Hodgson is happy to report that Jack has continued to grow in stature, if not wisdom, and has reached the ripe old age of three. The two of them live with their family in

Michigan, where Alison is at work on her first book about motherhood and shame. She also enjoys speaking and can be heard telling all the gory details about spirituality and writing at Breathe: A Christian Writer's Workshop. See www. breatheconference.com.

Roberta Hupprich is a retired United Methodist missionary who served as a nurse in Africa. Her work included a feeding program for street children in the Democratic Republic of Congo (Zaire) and the inception of a community based AIDS clinic in Zimbabwe where she cared for many orphans. She has four adult children and three grandchildren. Roberta lives at Penney Retirement Community in Florida with her husband, Glenn . . . and Rex.

After leaving the Indiana farm of his childhood, **Paul Ingram** became a newspaper photographer, writer, and editor. Today he works as a freelance writer and book editor. Paul graduated from Covenant Theological Seminary, St. Louis, Missouri, with a degree in historical theology, and his writings include a modern language paraphrase of Augustine's *Confessions, An Historian's Handbook to the Presbyterian Church in America*, and the historical novel *Children of the Mist*. He and his wife, Sheila, live in Grand Rapids, Michigan.

Millie Martin writes fiction and nonfiction for children and adults. Her publishing credits include fiction for children's magazines, curriculum materials, and devotions. She is a member of the Society of Children's Book Writers and Illustrators. When not writing, Millie enjoys reading, browsing antique shops, and gardening—an adult excuse to dig in the dirt. Visit her website, www.millietheismartin.com, for more information about her current writing projects.

Richard Meserva is a personal trainer, professional masseur, former body builder, and photographer. His dog Bo passed away soon after the writing of this story. Now Richard and his wife, Dawn, have a new friend—a lively pit bull mix from the pound named Smedley.

Award-winning author **Judythe Morgan** belongs to American Christian Fiction Writers and Romance Writers of America. Her publishing credits include articles, curriculum, devotionals, and selections in fiction and nonfiction works. When not writing, Judythe can be found browsing antique shops or walking her dogs . . . a very large Old English sheepdog and a very tiny Maltese. For more information about her current writing projects, Judythe encourages you to visit her website: www.judythemorgan.com.

Brooke Nolen has worked in book publishing for over thirteen years with Baker Publishing Group, InterVarsity Press, and Tyndale House Publishers. She is currently a master of divinity student at Grand Rapids Theological Seminary. She lives in Western Michigan in the company of her wheaten terrier and tabby cat, whose boxing and wrestling matches make homework time interesting.

Max Parks is the writer of many books.

Chris Pedersen and her husband live with a chocolate Lab named Brandy in the beautiful Sierra foothills of California. With two grown children and three grandchildren, Chris turned her career of writing technical material—from manuals to magazine articles—into writing for children. She is working on her second picture book and enjoys crafting nonfiction stories from real life. Her article "Work and Wag" appeared in Focus on the Family's *Clubhouse Jr.* magazine. Visit her blog at pawsandponder.blogspot.com.

Virginia Smith is the author of more than a dozen Christian novels and over fifty articles and short stories. An avid reader with eclectic tastes in fiction, Ginny writes in a variety of styles, from lighthearted relationship stories to breath-snatching suspense. She and her husband divide their time between Kentucky and Utah and escape as often as they can for "research trips" (or so she says) to scuba dive in the warm waters of the Caribbean. Learn more about Ginny and her books at www.VirginiaSmith.org.

Dorothy C. Snyder is a freelance writer and author from Jefferson City, Tennessee. She has published a number of articles in inspirational and secular magazines, and she is the author of a book titled *Our Journey through Alzheimer's: One Caregiver's Story.* Dorothy is a mother and grandmother who enjoys reading and spending time with her family.

Award-winning author **Pamela S. Thibodeaux** is the co-founder of Bayou Writers Group in Lake Charles, Louisiana. Multipublished in romantic fiction as well as in creative nonfiction, her writing has been tagged as "Inspirational with an Edge!" and reviewed as "steamier and grittier than the typical Christian novel *without* decreasing the message." See her website at www.pamelathibodeaux.com and her blog at pamswildroseblog.blogspot.com.

219

Sally Tolentino is the author of the book *My Eyes Have Seen Thy Glory* and the editor of the book *Fire in the Core*, as well as a contributing writer for other books and publications. When not writing, she is busy designing and sewing one-of-a-kind purses for her business, Via dei Fiori. Her love for animals is apparent not only in her writings but in her purse themes as well. She lives on a small farm in South Carolina with her husband of forty years, her miniature daschund Tico, and her two retired show horses. Visit her website at www.viadeifiori.com.

Shanna Verbecken is the mom of four grown children and grandmother of six grandsons. She lives in a new home since the fire, and she still has her dog Ladybug by her side. Shanna recently received her engagement ring from her fiancé, Bob, who has taken a job that doesn't require him to travel. They plan to be married very soon.

Barbara Warner holds a PhD in public policy from the University of Arkansas and is an assistant professor of political science at Arkansas State University. Prior to her academic career, she was a political science fellow, a legislative aide, and a press secretary for five members of Congress and the US House Small Business Committee. She also served the Clinton administration as a senior adviser for communications at the US Commerce Department. She has been a political journalist and a newspaper columnist.

Cathy E. Watkins was born an Earnhardt and loves NASCAR racing. She is a wife, mother of two, and grandmother of four who has been married to her husband, Mike, for twenty-seven years. Cathy loves all animals and people, including strangers. In fact, she says, "I get along with 'strange' very well!" This is her first published piece, although she contributed to the writing of the book *Pit Stop in a Southern Kitchen*, coauthored by her mother, Martha Earnhardt, and Carol Bickford.

Inspiring true stories of the dogs we love.

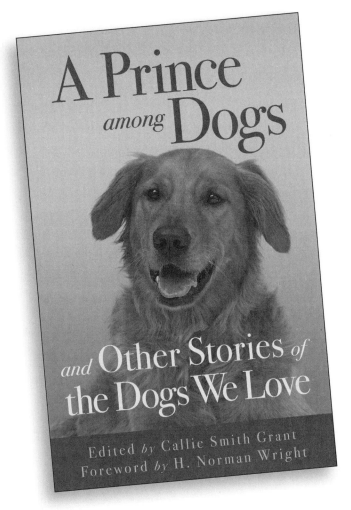

Heartwarming true stories of the cats we love.

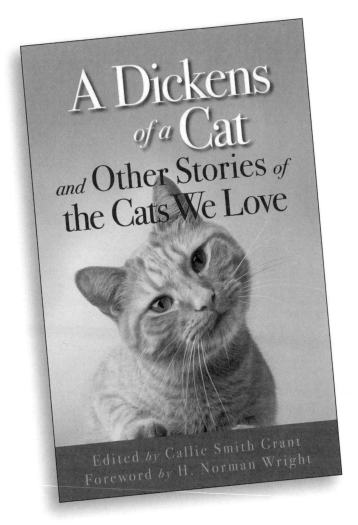

A Dickens *of a* Cat *and* Other Stories *of* the Cats We Love

Edited *by* Callie Smith Grant
Foreword *by* H. Norman Wright

 Revell
a division of Baker Publishing Group
www.RevellBooks.com

Available Wherever Books Are Sold